WORKING COWBOYS

DOUGLAS KENT HALL

WORKING COWBOYS

HOLT, RINEHART AND WINSTON
New York

Copyright © 1984 by Douglas Kent Hall
Published by Holt, Rinehart and Winston,
383 Madison Avenue, New York, New York 10017.
Published simultaneously in Canada by Holt, Rinehart
and Winston of Canada, Limited.

Library of Congress Cataloging in Publication Data
Hall, Douglas Kent.
Working cowboys.
1. Cowboys—West (U.S.)   2. Ranch life—West (U.S.)
3. West (U.S.)—Social life and customs.   I. Title.
F596.H26   1984   978   84-6630
ISBN Hardbound: 0-03-070417-0
ISBN Paperback: 0-03-070418-9

First Edition

Designer: Jacqueline Schuman
Printed in the United States of America
1 3 5 7 9 10 8 6 4 2

ISBN 0-03-070417-0 HARDBOUND

ISBN 0-03-070418-9 PAPERBACK

Frontispiece:
Royce Griggs, Ralph Hager, Terry Pilley

Acknowedgments page:
Gathering cattle, Frying Pan Ranch

This book is for Devon

My thanks to all the cowboys I met whose hospitality was immediate and genuine and whose generosity was boundless. I am especially grateful to the following:

Robert O. Anderson, Phil and Phillip Bidegan, Ninia Ritchie Bivins, John and Stanley Blackburn, Bobby and Betty Boston, Jenks Boston, Drummond and Diana Hadley, Don and Abby Hoffman, Richard and Kristen Holmes, Jim Humphries, Jeff Lane, Stanley Marsh, Bill O'Brien, Montie Richie, Willis Sheets, Bill and Becky Shepard, Steve Trigg, John and Susan Tull, and Jim Whittenburg IV.

ACKNOWLEDGMENTS

Harley Longan

WORKING COWBOYS

There was a morning when I understood how it all finally came together, how the new worked with the old, how there was a definite sense of something lost, and how that sense somehow finally did not matter any more. . . .

It is 4:00 A.M., in early May. I sit in a swaying 4×4 truck with Bobby and Jenks Boston, on the way to a ranch tucked away back in the hill country southwest of Clarendon, Texas. Coffee from an all-night convenience store on U.S. 287 sloshes in a Styrofoam cup, warming my hands, gradually bringing me awake.

The sky is still pitch black, with enough lightning exploding through the distant clouds brooding over Childress or Lubbock to keep the first talk of the morning confined to the weather and the chance that the day's branding might have to be called off. Jenks searches the radio for a weather report. A farm newscaster begins quoting the prices for cattle on the early market. Bobby reaches and turns it off. His voice grates, "We sure as hell don't need that."

Once we leave the pavement the truck shudders back and forth in the hard ruts left by the recent rains and the horse trailer rattles and lurches fitfully against the hitch. Out before us the hazy red taillights of other pickups and trailers flicker through the heavy boiling dust. "There's Jim," Jenks says, "and Donnie." Then, gradually, as the dust grows thicker and the lights seem to fade, the whole thing becoming increasingly more dreamlike, I feel that we are being transported farther and farther back from the present until, in fact, time no longer makes any difference.

The road snakes down to Sandy Camp, a collection of buildings hidden in a grove of trees. The dark yard in front of the house is parked full of pickups. Restless horses that were saddled by starlight over an hour ago snort and shift against the sides of the close trailers. Men in spurs stomp up the steps to the door. They leave their big hats in a pile in the corner of the living room, nod at each other, and disappear into the kitchen to get a cup of coffee. They all drink it black. "Spur juice," one young puncher calls it, motioning for me to grab a cup.

Opposite: Les Shannon

Johnny Hill is the camp man. With his family, he lives on this part of the ranch and is responsible for the cattle in these pastures. The word you first think when you meet Johnny is *straight*. He stands that way, tall and strong, a powerful-looking man with a definite set to his jaw. The only thing that throws the whole image out of balance is the wad of chewing tobacco that bulges in his right cheek and makes a little white spot in the skin.

Mrs. Hill hurries about the kitchen, busy cooking, something she has obviously been doing for the past hour and a half. She is fixing breakfast for fifteen men with big appetites. There are eggs, bacon, ham, grits, biscuits and gravy, big platters of everything steaming on the kitchen table.

Hill's daughter, Karen, a pretty, trim girl of about thirteen, her blond hair done in double ponytails, is already wearing her chaps, or leggings as they are called in this part of Texas, and a pair of spurs. I exchange a look with the cowboy sitting next to me. He waits until the girl leaves the room, then in a low voice says, "Johnny Hill never had no boys so he's done the best he could with his girls." He grins. "This one's about half monkey." I am not sure what he means until later in the day when the work is done, dinner eaten, and I see her pull off her boots and begin to perform a series of gracefully executed movements on the trampoline.

Once the food is ready Johnny urges the others to eat before it gets cold. He

Tom Blasingame, JA Ranch

will wait until last, which is part of the simple etiquette that still governs these men's lives. The cowboys, who have spoken little, grow totally silent while they eat. They never linger long over food. When their plates are empty they carry them to the sink in the kitchen. On the way out they murmur quietly to Mrs. Hill, "I enjoyed it," the words softened in the broad accent Panhandle people have. Then they pick up their hats and slip outside to wait.

Each man looks at the sky, though now there isn't much to say about the weather. To the south the clouds are still banked in a high, dark wall but the winds seem to be driving them steadily away; the play of lightning has diminished to an occasional flash and the throaty thunder no longer rumbles its way along the distant horizon.

Young boys, sons and grandsons of the camp men and the neighboring cowboys who've come to help, are huddled together under the porch light. They pass a tin of Copenhagen like a vague sacrament. The youngest, whose name is Tuffy and who couldn't be any older than six or seven, crowds up to get his share. Already the round snuff cans have worn badgelike circles in the hind pockets of most of their jeans. They step to the edge of the porch and send long streams of the juice over the rail. Recalling a day I spent so sick from a chew of tobacco I wanted to die, I question one boy about it. "Naw, this ain't nothing like that," he says,

The Remuda, Bell Ranch

Opposite: Brian Thomas

spitting importantly out into the grass. "A pinch of snuff's like candy."

Though it is still dark when the cowboys start to move out of the yard, the sky in the east is beginning to glow with soft morning colors. The pickups with their trailers travel in a caravan along the rough dirt track to a set of pens at the head of a wild pasture containing a few thousand acres. In the next three hours the cowboys will circle and gather it, hunting the cattle out of the brush and bringing them back to this point, where they will be worked—the calves castrated, vaccinated, and branded, and the whole herd sprayed. The entire operation will be over by noon.

The horses are unloaded and the riders get mounted. Suddenly, outlined against the red morning sky, they become startling figures. The men sit their horses and speak in hushed, almost reverent voices. Johnny Hill gives directions for the drive. Then the riders begin to move toward the ridge. A spur rings and is dulled against a horse's belly. A steel shoe turns a stone. Mesquite thorns pick at the hard leather shell of a man's chaps with a sound like tearing paper.

4

Arlyn Norman

Tom Blasingame

6

On the top of the low ridge, horses and riders appear to pause for a moment, stern single figures cast hard against the sunrise. With the trucks behind me and the barbed wire almost invisible in the murky dark that still clings close to the earth, I feel suddenly transported back in time—a hundred years, more—a man privileged to watch the beginning of some magic spectacle. Then, in the next instant, with no warning, the cowboys are gone, plunging down into the wild country after the cows, leaving in their wake a complete and perfect silence.

We can only speculate about how he began, and where. The first cowboy could have been some luckless Spanish youth whose dreams of glory as a great conqueror and soldier of fortune went awry and left him looking for a job.

Let's assume he was a kid who ran away from his home in rural Spain, found his way down to a port city, and shipped out as a cabin boy, hoping never to spend another day working on the family farm. It is easy to imagine how his spirits plunged when he heard that his primary job on board was taking care of livestock. He had to feed the cattle and horses and see that they had their meager ration of water. Then he had to rake the shit from their stalls and pitch it to the fish that schooled behind the slow schooner as it rode the winds to the New World.

This is sheer conjecture, of course, but it is conceivable that there was a point at which the cabin boy actually abandoned his desire to sign on with the soldiers or stay with the ship and asked to be left in Santo Domingo to work the cows. It could be that he decided there was more continuity to taking care of cattle than riding off to war.

Later, then, he was the young man who prodded the offspring of those same beasts up the ramp and into the ship Gregorio de Villalobos took from Cuba to what would eventually become Mexico. Moving with the cattle as their keeper and protector had become his life. He swam them through the surf to the beach and drove them into the tall grass along the Panuco River.

Later still, seasoned, far more experienced, and already developing a style and an expertise, he found work as a *vaquero* on the big spread Hernan Cortez called Cuernavaca. He drew from a fire the glowing iron brand of three Christian crosses and burned it into the hide of a bellowing Cuernavaca calf, thus leaving on that creature's rump what appears to have been the first brand on this continent.

Something must have set the *vaquero* apart from the other more mundane men of that day whose lives revolved around tending animals and tilling the soil—farmers, dairymen, sheepherders. Perhaps it was having observed what glorious figures the conquistadores cut, mounted on their sturdy horses and decked out in fine gear and gleaming armor, that brought him up from the dirt, so to speak, and onto the back of a horse, to travel the way they traveled.

The gear he gradually either invented himself or adopted from the conquistadores was, of course, largely functional; it was made up of the basic tools he needed to accomplish his task. But what of the bits of fancy braiding, the stamping, the occasional piece of etched silver that kept cropping up among his gear? Were they essential to carrying out what always before had been considered a lowly enterprise? Did this *vaquero* need conchos and fancy inlay to turn a stampeding herd? Did the boots he eventually wore require decoration to keep his feet fast in his stirrups? Were the big spurs with rowels like stars necessary to ride horses already so spirited and bred full of fire that they were usually hard to hold?

Vaquero. The word has a sound that says it can accommodate all of the extravagances of the man. From the Spanish, it translates roughly as cowboy. Twisted into the accent of the Northwest when the cow people up there took the word into their own peculiar lingo it became buckaroo. Cowpuncher is supposedly the name he earned when he started prodding cows with a pole in his attempts to load them into stock cars after the drive to the railroads in the midwest. It is plausible, historically correct, and probably even true. But the story I prefer involves a cowboy who was just setting a red hot branding iron to the hide of a big yearling steer when it jerked a foot loose and proceeded to kick the cowboy clear across the corral; the cowboy picked himself up, ran over to the steer, and punched the sorry creature in the jaw with such sheer force he knocked him cold. Cowpuncher.

Some people, especially those inclined to the romantic, like to think of the cowboy as rootless. They see him as a shiftless creature who somehow emerged full-blown and fully formed and dressed exactly as we see him now—in hat, chaps, boots, and spurs—and in the saddle riding. They don't credit Mexico with any part of it and in their eyes he can have no Spanish, Indian, Mestizo, or Mexican blood flowing in his veins. They place his origins somewhere in Texas and believe it is all right if he doesn't care to tell exactly where he really was born.

If it was Texas, then at least some of what transpired there was anything but flattering to the image or the man. Early in the nineteenth century, roughly 300 years after the first *vaqueros* began working in Mexico, bands of Texans were slipping across the border to steal cattle. They rode mostly at night and had their best luck when there was a full moon. They would stampede a large Mexican herd and then run as many head as they could back through the Rio Grande into Texas, where the animals were sold for their hides or used as breeding stock.

Wherever he began and whatever he was called, cowboy, buckaroo, cowpuncher, or any of the numerous names that fell to him within the ranks of his profession, the man flourished and his numbers grew. His world became a haven and a hiding place for the wanted, the unwanted, the strange, and the eccentric. It welcomed the drifter, the loner, and the man who claimed no past, as well as the man with more past than he cared to acknowledge.

In the stereotype, the cowpuncher is usually pictured as a patient, quiet man who likes to keep to himself and has an affinity for the animals he hired on to raise and protect—except when he is in town, of course; then he is depicted as wild, crude, unruly, quarrelsome, and sometimes downright mean—a holy terror.

Sometimes cowboys did do a little damage. But ordinarily it wasn't intentional. Most often they were merely hard-working boys out to let off a little steam.

Leo Turner remembers one of those times when they were trying to have some fun;
it started innocently enough but everything kept going haywire. "Old Jerry Allen
and I was working south of Guthrie, Texas, on the Bar J G. We rode horseback to
Girard where we'd heard they was having a dance out in the country. We got there
and all these kids who was friends of ours had already gone. Some of them had
Model T's and whatnot. Jerry got to drinking, which was something he was pretty
handy at. It was during prohibition and he was drinking pear extract, I believe. You

Hands, T O Ranch

9

could buy that out of the drugstore. We got our hair cut and Jerry said we was going to find a way to get to that dance."

Sitting at the counter in his daughter's kitchen, the heels of his boots hooked over the rung on his stool, Leo stops and takes a sip of hot chocolate. He is a big man with a rough, weathered face and keen, clear eyes. "There was this one little old street that went through Girard, just a dirt road that went north and turned east and then cut back north again. Jerry was just drunk as a hoot owl and wearing this brand new pair of boots. This old Overland car with these old people from out of state was coming and Jerry ran out in the street in front of them, waving his arms and trying to flag them down. You know, he thought it was somebody who lived there. They didn't know what to think. Here was this drunk flapping his arms and acting like he wanted to get hisself killed, and they got scared and started trying to dodge him.

"These old Overland cars had springs that stick way out in front at an angle"—Leo draws it out in the air with his hands—"and kind of join to something out there. Finally Jerry jumped right in front of the car and them old springs knocked him down. When it run over him that old car bounced as high as this counter."

Leo slaps the Formica top and brays with laughter. "It tore the sole off one of his new boots, ripped it off plumb down to the heel and left the sole flapping. We gathered Jerry up and took him into the back of the drugstore and laid him out on a table. I went after Doc Wilkerson. Old Doc had known Jerry all his life and when

he saw who it was he said, 'Drunk, just drunk,' and turned around to go out. This feller with me named Yates said, 'Doc, you big-bellied so-and-so, a car run over him.' Doc said, 'He's just drunk.' I thought we was going to have to whip old Doc to make him examine Jerry, who was still out cold. Doc felt him over. He didn't have a broke bone in his body. He was just bruised, but his boots sure looked awful. We finally got him to come to. They put us up in the rooming house that night. We got up the next morning, wrapped a piece of baling wire around Jerry's ruined boot, and headed back to the Bar J G. We never did get to that dance."

Rootless he probably was. But often he maintained that attitude of rootlessness, of being free to roll his bed and move, on a single spread. It was a kind of independence that was as much a part of the image as the boots and big hat he wore and Bull Durham cigarettes he rolled to smoke. Two prime examples are Gail Chacon at the Trigg Ranch and Tom Blasingame at the JA Ranch. After their initial wandering from ranch to ranch as young cowboys they have both stayed on the same pay list for over fifty years, though they still might deny that what they are holding down is a permanent job.

If the idea of independence has always been an important and fiercely guarded commodity to a puncher, so too has his image, his visual image. It has been said that contrary to all claims of how functional most of his gear is, the cowboy chooses his costume more for the shadow it helps him cast than for any other more practical reason. In *Trails Plowed Under*, Charles M. Russell, the painter, wrote: "Cow-

punchers were mighty particular about their rig, an' in all the camps you'd find a fashion leader. From a cowpuncher's idea, these fellers was sure good to look at, an' I tell you right now, there ain't no prettier sight for my eyes than one of those good-lookin', long-backed cowpunchers, sittin' up on a high-forked, full-stamped California saddle with a live hoss between his legs."

More than one young cowboy admitted to me that the image, the way you look and feel, is one compensation in a trade where a man works long hours for short pay. In my own past there were hundreds of winter nights after chores when I would spend hours avoiding homework while I pored over the hat and boot pages of Miller Stockmen, Montgomery Ward, and Sears catalogues—comparing the qualities of Stetson and Resistol, of Justin, Nocona, Tony Lama, Hyer. So in a limited way, then, I suppose I can understand what it is that drives a young cowboy to look to tradition for his basic direction and then add some frills of his own.

One of those stylish punchers who come to mind is Sam McDonald. His handmade boots had black French calf vamps with full-stitched slick high red patent leather tops and he wore Mexican silver spurs with big spikey rowels; he had on a dark vest, there was a pure silk wild-rag knotted at his throat, and he wore heavy leather cuffs that reached from his wrists to his elbows; his hat, with its uncreased crown, was decorated out with a band and stampede string of finely braided horsehair; and the whole thing was finished off with a pair of black silk arm bands.

A cowboy is at least as particular about the equipment he puts on his horse as he is about what he wears himself. The considerations are safety, comfort, and style—and though they should be in that order, there are cowboys who would reverse it. Like clothing, the equipment changes from area to area, from cowboy to cowboy.

The saddle used by the contemporary puncher is still only a variation on the saddles brought to the New World by the conquistadores; they had, in turn, taken as their model the war saddles ridden by the Moors. The earliest changes in the configuration of saddles were dictated partly by the use to which it was put by the *vaqueros* and later the cowboys and partly by the materials available to the saddlemaker (in the beginning this was very often the *vaquero* or cowboy himself).

Like the saddle, the bit used in a horse's mouth to give the rider control came the same route through Mexico from Spain, where it was probably introduced by the Moors, who invaded the Visigothic kingdom of Roderick in 711. The basic design of the bit—a steel rod through the mouth—has been embellished upon numerous times either out of fancy or need. The two outside pieces to which the headstall and the reins are fastened have often been decorated up with silver and occasionally gold to the point of sheer gaudiness. There are gentle bits and cruel bits, ranging from the snaffle to the spade. Some punchers maintain any bit is unnecessarily cruel and won't ride with a bit; others won't ride without one. Why they are chosen and how they are used usually tells a great deal more about the man than the horse.

No real working man has ever been the sole model for a greater hero than the cowboy. There isn't any really plausible or concrete explanation for his popularity. The cowboy just happened. And he has been America's biggest single contribution to the myth and literature of the world, a figure that has surpassed any other hero out of any other country or culture. He had his predecessors, to be sure, though they seem not to have been his models. Once, the kind of man who became a cowboy in America and rode the rough string might have fought under King Arthur and the great warrior kings of Europe; and, in an earlier age, he might have gone to wander the seas with men like Ulysses. Somewhere in his evolution there was some kind of alchemy; it was as if by magic a base metal had been turned to gold.

There is, of course, a similarity between the knight and the sailor and the cowboy, but there is also a distinct difference. Something about the combination of cattle and vast tracts of land that seemed fit for no use beyond grazing attracted men of a certain spirit and produced a unique kind of individual and consequently a uniquely different hero. The reason for this is probably that he is unlike the knight who, when he steps down from his charger, becomes a creaking, ungainly figure; and he is unlike the sailor who, when he leaves his ship, is pretty much the same as any other man. The cowboy, the "sure-enough" cowboy, as punchers like to say in reference to the genuine article, doesn't exactly diminish when he kicks his right

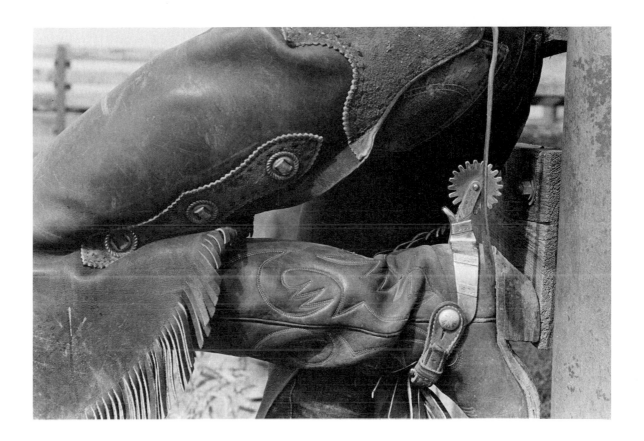

foot from the stirrup and swings to the ground. He has a look that sets him apart from other, more ordinary men. You notice him in the saddle and you can sure pick him out on the street.

In his book *The West from a Car-Window*, published in 1892, Richard Harding Davis wrote: "The cowboy cannot be overestimated as a picturesque figure; all that has been written about him and all the illustrations that have been made of him fail to familiarize him, and to spoil the picture he makes when one sees him for the first time racing across a range outlined against the sky, with his handkerchief flying out behind, his sombrero bent back by the wind, and his gauntlets and broad leather leggings showing above and at the side of his galloping pony. And his deep seat in the saddle, with his legs hanging straight to the long stirrups, the movement of his body as it sways and bends, and his utter unconsciousness of the animal beneath him would make a German riding-master, and English jockey, or the best cross-country rider of the Long Island hunting club shake his head in envy and despair."

A contemporary cowboy is picturesque in his own way. Studied, often out-rageous in spite of that traditional cowboy reserve, he is authentic. Douglas E. Johnson from the T O Ranch put it this way: "You stand out in a crowd. You can go to town and see a lot of them urban-type cowboys that walk around in boots and hats and everything, but when you see a sure-enough cowboy walk down the street

1 5

he's got a little swagger to his walk and his hat don't look near as pretty as some of them that just walked out of the store. You can just spot a riding hand pretty quick."

The North American cowboy was scarcely fifty years old when his death notices began rolling in. The earliest statement I read that the cowboy as a breed was dying out came in an article published in *Scribner's Magazine*, the June issue of 1892. The journalist, Charles Moreau Harger, states somewhere near the end of his piece: "The cow-boy with his white, wide-brimmed hat, his long leathern cattle whip, his lariet, and his clanking spur is a thing of the past." And he concludes: ". . . and like the cavalier, the troubadour, the Puritan, and the 'Forty-niner,' the cow-boy and his attendant life have become but figures in history."

Almost sixty years later John Bryson, in his text for Leonard McCombe's book of photographs, *The Cowboy*, featuring C.H. Long, the range boss of the JA Ranch, states: "Men like C.H., in general appearance not much unlike Texas cowboys of a century ago, constitute America's greatest single contribution to the romantic folklore of the world, as Europe's is the armored, mounted knight. On the great ranches, the horse is making his last stand in America as a working animal, and unmechanized outfits like the JA are growing rare. The pictures in this book are perhaps a final honest look at a life that is disappearing and a vanishing breed of rugged, skillful men."

And in recent years, after the cowboy has been in existence in Texas and points north for at least a century and a half and has established himself as one of the major figures in both the real world and the world of myth, a figure upon whose style whole industries have been based, Harger's statement and the cry of those who followed him are still being echoed by intelligent and observant men who ought to know better. Books with titles that read like epitaphs continue to be published. What they seem to be, however, are largely photographic works that present strong evidence in the number of photographs of young, incredibly authentic-looking cowpunchers that the cowboy is, in fact, an enduring breed.

Mention the notion that his kind is fast becoming a thing of the past to a cowboy on one of the big working ranches west of Mosquero, New Mexico, and he'll push his chair back from the supper table, his big spurs clanking on the linoleum, shake his head, and declare that that's a matter of opinion. "I sure don't think they're dying out. I think there's more cowboys now than there ever was. I think there'll be a different kind of cowboy in years to come because automation is slowly but surely moving into the cow business. But it won't ever take over. Some of these places are just too big and rough to run without cowboys, like the Bell Ranch. You're going to have to have horseback cowboys to run it like it's got to be worked. There's no kind of vehicle you can invent that can do what a horse can do. There's a lot of people that are in the cow business because they love it; and their kids'll be in it and their grandkids'll be in it. Like my boy Jason. I think it's imbedded in him enough that he'll be in some branch of the cattle industry. It's pretty hard on a kid his age but it

Opposite: Gary Green

1 7

Tom Sparks, Joe Shadle, Gary Gregory

Jack Chatfield

gets easier as you get older. You learn to cope. You learn all the shortcuts. You have to worry a lot. You're under a lot of pressure. They expect a fifteen-year-old boy to do a man's work and that's a lot of pressure on a kid. The older you get, the easier it gets, and the easier it gets, the more you want to stay."

In spite of the encroachment of technology, much of which has yet to prove its superior value, cowboys still exist; to some extent, in fact, their existence has been strengthened because of this technology, because it has shown that finally they cannot be replaced. Today's cowboys, like their historical counterparts, have learned to adjust to the changes that continue to creep into their lives. They take the bitter with the sweet. And they get on horseback as much as they can.

Hands such as Sam McDonald, Stevie Chacon, Bo Cribbs, Hershel Stone, Mike Martin, and Jason Eicke are being born into it and want no other life. Other men are coming into the business the way outsiders have always been lured into it—through dreams and fantasies. Doug Johnson is one of the latter kind of young cowboys. "I grew up in town, up there in Kansas," he told me one day in the saddle room on the T O. "I got started reading a lot of Will James books. I liked everything he did—the way he wrote and the way he drew. And I decided that this was the way I was going to spend my time, just punching cows."

Roger Long, who was raised in a cowboy family in the heart of the Panhandle, decided he'd try something else, to see if he couldn't find a life that suited him better. "My dad, he was a cowboy. I had four brothers and we just grew up thinking that's the only thing there was to be. I done three or four different things after I got out of high school. I worked for the fire department. Then I was in the service. I worked at a gas refinery. I found out that I didn't like nothing but cowboying. I wasn't near as happy anyplace else as I am out here in these hills and open flats."

Lafe Popejoy is a lean, shy cowboy as laconic as they come, a classic example of the breed. When I ask Lafe why he stays on the ranch, doing his own work, day-working bigger outfits to make ends meet, he looks me in the eyes and spells it out: "It's a good clean life." To Lafe that's not only important, it's everything.

The truth is that cowboys have shown little resistance to progress, at least to the kind of progress that seems to work—either to improve their own lives or the lives of the cattle they have hired on to raise and maintain. Inventions such as the squeeze-chute and calf-table, devices that supposedly make branding, dehorning, castrating, and vaccinating easier for the cowboy and less traumatic for the cattle, were at one time going to revolutionize the business. Against their better judgment, cowboys gave them a chance. Now they are being questioned not only by cowboys but by many ranch owners and managers. On almost every big ranch I visited I saw calf-tables and squeeze-chutes. In most cases they had grown full of grass and weeds and showed little evidence of extensive use. Only once did I see one in operation and that was on a purebred Hereford ranch near Wichita Falls, Texas. It did, however, seem appropriate for that particular job, doctoring heifers for pinkeye.

A cowboy in a corral near Santa Rosa, New Mexico, nods toward a calf-table just recently added to a long chute and curses. "I think I'd rather have a couple of men holding me down than to be squeezed up between a couple of cold steel grids." He grins and adds that his favorite part of spring work is dragging calves—roping them by both hind feet and dragging them to the branding fire, traditional cowboy work.

Leo Turner speaks bluntly. "I wouldn't have a calf-table if they give it to me. What experience I've had, it took about as many men to run one as it did to work cattle the old way. I don't think it's easy on the calf. You've got to squeeze the heck out of them. I flanked about twelve hundred calves through one of those things on the Ladder Ranch and by the time we was through I hated it. You do a better job on the ground. Besides, if they use them calf-tables they'll never have any more cowboys. What if he has to go out and rope a calf?"

On the T O Ranch outside of Raton, New Mexico, Gary Loveland turns from saddling his horse and says, "One of the first things I ask—before I even ask what the wages is going to be—is if they have a calf-table or a squeeze-chute. If they do, I don't want the job. Those things are hard on men and they're harder on cattle and they take about twice the time to get the same work done."

Of all the changes that have come into the cowboy life the one with the most profound impact has been the pickup. It has almost completely done away with what some men feel was the greatest cowboy institution, the chuckwagon. Like mesquite and sagebrush, which were replaced by propane gas for branding fires, the chuckwagon and all it represented fell in the name of a better way—progress. A few big outfits with stubborn management still take the wagon out for a few weeks a year, a few others whose owners and managers have come to question the dubious wisdom of abandoning a great tradition are now considering running one again. And maybe they will—not only for the sake of nostalgia, but for the sake of the life.

On the positive side, the pickup has made feasible the practice of neighboring, where cowboys from various outfits trade work with other ranches in the same vicinity; this has the advantage of giving each ranch a substantial crew during high work times such as branding and shipping, and makes it so they don't have to carry a great number of cowboys on the pay list during the slack periods. In this way a compromise is reached. The cowboy life goes on and ranches forced to operate within the microscopically narrow margins of today's cattle business are able to make ends meet. Cowboys are pretty patient. They give a little and keep a little and sometimes if they wait a little they can take back a little.

Most punchers are not unreasonable. They recognize the value of the pickups they drive and how useful they are in their line of work. They tolerate them for that reason but they hate them all the same; they hate them for what they have done to the world where they live.

"The main difference between us and cowboys of the past," a Texas cowboy says, summing it up, "is the hours spent ahorseback. I think we do things pretty much the same way they used to back then. These days we've got pickups and trailers and in the old days they wore out more horses and saddle leather. I'd sooner have the old way. I'd sooner be ahorseback any day than I would be driving around in that damned pickup."

The pickup has affected not only the hours a man spends mounted, it has changed the quality of the horses he rides. "There's just no way you can make a horse by pulling him around in a trailer," Doug Johnson states. "I think the more miles he gets on him the better kind of horse he's going to be. Pickups have brought about a new breeding. Horses aren't like they used to be. The stockier built quarter horses we use today can't take as many miles as the older, more thoroughbred-looking horses did. He won't last near as long. If you trotted him fifteen or twenty miles to get to where you was working he'd be sure enough wore out, where the longer muscled thoroughbred-type horse would still be under you and he'd carry you back home."

Changes were inevitable. They took their toll on certain aspects of the old life. Still, most punchers are optimists. Very few of them seem particularly concerned that the machine is ever going to do much of the work or that the cowboy is doomed to die. Men with newfangled ideas out of college classrooms have come into ranching and tried to work cattle in other ways. Dick Foster has seen it. "A lot of college men are taking over these ranches now and they're trying to do it the real

modern way with all this modern machinery and stuff but it doesn't work. It may take a while but I think we're going to see a little turnaround. They'll be going back to the old way. It's cheaper and it's the best."

The new breed of ranch managers have used helicopters, airplanes, pickups, motorcycles, and various other nameless, jerry-built four-wheel-drive contraptions to work cattle. This craziness has neither discouraged cowboys nor driven them into the unemployment lines.

"I think there'll always be cowboys," says Roger Long. "I don't think you can breed it out of some men. It's in them. If they're going to have cows and horses you're going to have to have somebody to look after them. You can't do it by machine. I don't think there's a way to replace a horse and a man. A lot of people try to do it with motorcycles and helicopters. I've seen a lot of them try to do it on them little old three-wheelers but they don't get the job done." A sheepish look crosses his face. "It'd be kind of hard to rope off one of them things, wouldn't it?"

They call it Casa Colorado, a cow camp on the north end of the sprawling Bell Ranch, out where the magic of New Mexico begins to take over after the vast expanses of the Texas Panhandle have played out and the country has become a little wilder, a little rougher.

Just before dawn, with a sliver of moon and the morning star hanging above the mesa that thrusts up abruptly to the east, the yellow stuccoed adobe house is bathed in a strange, eerie light. Jim Eicke, his big roweled spurs already alive on the flagstone steps, slips outside, his first morning coffee steaming in a white mug. Jim stands over six feet tall and seen in silhouette, wearing a black "7-high-5" Resistol hat, dusted and shaped by an indeterminate number of hard seasons, he looms even larger, a legendary figure in a world of legends. His face, divided by an amazing blond mustache, is friendly; but something in the way his eyes can suddenly go cold tells you he could turn mean in, say, a fight with a puncher or anyone else who'd crossed him. Which might only be natural to a man whose work is hazardous, a man who bleeds a little almost every day—from mesquite, barbed wire, ropes, and all of the machines it takes to get his work done.

With each move Jim makes his spurs ring. Spurs have a long and sketchy history. It is said they were in use as early as the seventh century B.C. Then they were of a simple, utilitarian design meant merely to prod stubborn mounts into action. Later, they became a badge, a social accoutrement, and the honor to wear them was conferred by a king or some other dignitary of note. Possibly it was then that they became so decorated. They announced the presence of a knight or a cavalier. In South America, the rowels on the spurs worn by gauchos were sometimes called *Nazarenas* because in size and configuration they were like Christ's crown of thorns. With Jim, they are a tool—but they may also be a badge.

Morning is Jim's favorite time. In fact, the only possible improvement he can imagine upon this moment would be if he were already mounted and riding. "The best part of this life," he declares, drawing up his shoulders against the edge in the

Opposite: Stevie Chacon

breeze, "is being out on a nice cool early morning when there's a little frost on the ground, riding a good horse, watching the animals run and hearing the calves bawl." You can feel it in his voice—the crispness, the fresh smells of the range at daybreak, the smooth gait of a big horse that his son Jason has green-broke, that Jim has trained (as each cowboy does) to his own tastes and needs. "To me, that's just something. A lot of people probably wouldn't appreciate it, but I don't think you can beat it. It's about the best deal I've ever found." He holds his cup in both hands, savoring the warmth while he watches the colors play in the sky. "It's hard work, but I like hard work. You don't do the same thing every day. Some days it may be just as wild as spending the night in the Watts area of Los Angeles and then some days," he smiles, indicating that this is one of those days, "it's kind of slow." Down the draw from the house, the windmill creaks and begins to turn.

From the kitchen come the smells of breakfast. Jim's wife Sharon has the radio tuned to a station in Tucumcari or Las Vegas and is listening to Willie Nelson sing a Lefty Frizzell song. Jim chuckles, sucking on a cigarette. "Old Willie didn't always look as wild as he does now." He remembers the time in Lubbock or someplace when Willie signed an album and gave it to him. "He never had that pigtail in them days. Looked just like a preacher, wearing a suit and them pointy-toed shoes."

Sharon calls the kids a second time; they need to catch their school bus before seven for the long ride over rough dirt roads to other ranch camps before they end up in Roy, thirty miles away.

"I can tell you the worst part of cowboying, too," Jim says. He reaches and brushes the two sides of his mustache away from his mouth. "Windmilling and gathering bulls in the fall. If I carried a gun there wouldn't be a live bull on this place. I'd shoot every damn one of them, I guarantee you I would." His eyes crinkle. I can almost hear Jim's string of profanity as he begins to climb a windmill that needs repairing or painting. And I can see him drawing a bead on one of the big Herefords or a treacherous longhorn and blowing him into bull heaven. "I guess that's the hardest part of punching cows—gathering them damn bulls every fall."

He crushes his cigarette on the waist-high stone wall and then field-strips it. "And the money's not that good either. But I don't worry about the money. I always thought the reason a man worked was to give his family a decent place to live, plenty to eat, and to make a good home for them. We have all that right here. Hell, we don't need a lot of money. People say, God, you work for that much a month! But they don't look at the other side of it. What wages I get are mine. I don't have to pay no rent, no gas, no lights. I don't have to go to town and buy that high-priced beef."

Sharon has breakfast laid on the big Spanish colonial table Jason made last year in shop. She yells at the kids—hurry. Jason, a slight-built boy who already has a reputation as a cowboy and plays the guitar with a nice touch, is even quieter than usual. He has a problem. At school today they're going to shoot the yearbook pictures and the principal has forbidden him to wear his black Resistol, which is newer than Jim's and not as weathered. Jim looks up from his plate and says there's no solution, except to do what the man tells him. Certain things you have to learn to live with. Out front, the bus begins honking and they race for it, the screen slamming.

Sharon sighs and smiles, relaxing now that the kids are gone. She looks years younger than she is. She is beautiful in a natural way, with a complexion that seems too fair for this windy country. She was born on a farm in Texas and raised in a small town. She doesn't miss any of that. "This is the kind of life I always dreamed about," she says. "It's not something we just ended up doing."

Jim disappears onto the porch and returns with a bridle and a pair of new reins. While he talks about cowboying, he cuts off the old reins. He has done other things and seen a good bit of the world, and can talk knowledgeably about places like Hong Kong, Tokyo, L.A., New York, as well as cities in Europe. "We just keep coming back to this, knowing what it's like, how much it pays, what we have to do."

But this is not the real point. "I believe that out here you're a lot closer to your family. You do more things together—" Jim shakes his head and laughs. "When you

Shipping cattle, T4 Ranch

do do something it has to be all together. I believe that if more people'd do things that way the world would be a better place."

"That's true," Sharon agrees. She flashes a look at Jim, a little uneasy about what she wants to say. "There's times when you wish the sun would shine so he could go do something out away from the house a bit. But, all in all, it's the only way to live, the only way to raise kids. I know a lot of little kids being raised in the city and they don't have the same attitude as our kids. They take things for granted. All the things that are special to my kids are an everyday occurrence to city kids. There's nothing really special left for them. Our kids are learning to appreciate life. You have to like to be alone, which we are most of the time."

Jim holds one new rein on the bit, keeping his head turned to the side so the smoke from his cigarette will curl away from his eye. "One of the things I *like* about this work is being alone—which I am ninety percent of the time. I do enjoy going and working with the crew. When you're alone, though, it's a lot different. You do your own thinking. Nobody interrupts you. You see a lot of things you wouldn't see

Montie Richie

if you were with people. I wouldn't have it any other way. In the summertime, Jason is with me. But even then me and him will split up and be alone too." He pulls the ties through the holes in the rein with a pair of pliers and knots them securely. "I don't like being around a lot of people. They make me nervous. I start having to dig my Rolaids out." Cigarettes, too. "I usually just smoke three packs a day, but whenever I get around people I smoke five. I'll tell you what, we have to psych ourselves up just to go to town. All of us. It's real hard on me."

Which is different from what it was when all the big-time celluloid cowboys were having their heyday on the ranges around Hollywood. You rarely even saw any cattle. Hoppy, Hoot, Roy, Gene, Johnny Mack Brown, and all those guys in perfectly creased, tailored clothes were always saddling up and heading into town, riding through brush that wasn't even serious enough to scratch the shine off their boot toes, to a road that was better maintained than eighty percent of the ranch roads today. They'd hang out at the bar, tossing down shots of straight whiskey and winning at cards, until the girl arrived on a stage from the East or they'd run into some mean sonofabitch who was causing everybody trouble and needed killing.

Jim puts down the bridle long enough to light a fresh cigarette. "We usually go in once a month. Sharon has to buy groceries. Sometimes if I need some materials or something to work with I might just run in and buy it. Or if she runs a little low on some groceries she might go in. But other than going to the doctor or something like that we generally go once a month. And sometimes I don't go then. Sharon goes by herself. If you've ever been shopping with your wife, you know what that's like. If we're both going into town and she's got a lot of shopping to do we take two vehicles. She goes her way and I go mine. I don't like walking around them stores looking at clothes and things."

Sharon doesn't relish the trips to town any more than Jim does. As she puts it, "If I could snap my fingers and have my cabinets full of groceries I'd be happy. It would suit me to stay out here all the time." She brings the coffee pot to the table and fills our cups while she talks. "We have friends who are not cow people who cannot imagine that we rarely go to a movie, that we rarely go dancing, or do any of the things that they do. Not everyone can live this way, and a lot more people can't understand it. I guess it takes all kinds. I've lived in a city and didn't like it. I'm just one of the ones that happens to love living out here."

"It's eighty miles to Tucumcari," Jim says. "That's not far enough, really. I wish it was a hundred and eighty."

Ask Sharon if she isn't bothered by the isolation and she laughs. "Oh, no. I love it. I'm not a real social person. I've always been kind of private. I don't like clubs. I'm not even a member of the Cow Belles."

"You know," Jim coils the new reins with the headstall and drops the bridle beside his chair, "we're not near as isolated as we would have been back fifty or sixty years ago. We're two hours from town. But that don't seem like very far to be from all them people who're doing all them bad things to each other. If we want to go drink a beer we're not that far from a beer joint. Or we can go to the neighbor's and

play dominoes and I can get just as drunk sitting there at the kitchen table playing dominoes as I can down at one of them high-priced city bars. We get a lot of enjoyment out of simple things—like going to a picture show. We may go once every three months. And when we do we enjoy it a whole lot. If I lived where I could go every day I don't know whether I would even like it. Anybody burns out. Get enough chocolate pudding and you get to where you just hate that pudding."

A tremendous romanticism has grown up around the cowboy, much of it kept alive by people other than the cowboy himself, not the least of which are cowboy wives and families. So while Jim goes outside to load a few things into his pickup I ask Sharon why she, a girl from town, married a cowboy.

"As far back as I can remember," she says, "I was always attracted to cowboys. I don't know why it was. Their charm." She stops, then adds that it is also their sensitivity. "I think that cowboys have a special feeling for nature, an appreciation for life that is immediate. They see the babies, the calves, the renewal every spring

Harley Longan

of the grass and the wildflowers. I think it's just something about them that a lot of people don't have."

Heading into a large pasture to the south and west of the house Jim talks and drives, the rowels of his spurs ringing whenever he shifts gears or stabs at the brake. He loves his life, loves being a cowboy. It is a job with a badge like no other. The name cowboy—its simple and literal meaning aside—comes freighted with a history and a mythology that Jim and most of the other cowboys I've met seem determined to protect and perpetuate. What made Jim want to be a cowboy?

"My dad was a cowboy. My granddad was a cowboy. Granddad had a ranch in Snyder, Texas, but that's such dry country that he didn't do much good. He moved to Brownfield and started taking all the Santa Fe Railroad freight from Lubbock to Brownfield and from Brownfield to Seagraves. He had mules and wagons. My dad run off from home and went to work on a ranch. I grew up in it. It's just in my blood."

I had heard that same sentiment echoed in southern New Mexico, in Texas, in Nevada, in Colorado, Wyoming, Arizona. Gary Green had said it, so had Jim Robinson, Kelly Shannon, Floyd Sanders, and Harley Longan—cowboys who had come into the profession because it was the natural, expected thing to do. There were others, like Robbie Seale on the JA and Jim Whiteker on the T4, both city

Ricky Ortega and Billy Collard

boys, who had been attracted to it and had come into it after they were out of school.

Up ahead, a huge tarantula, standing so tall on its hairy legs that you can see it almost a hundred yards away, is starting across one of the ruts in the dirt track. Jim swerves a little to miss it and says that if they're starting to move it must be going to rain.

I ask what he thinks it takes to make a good cowboy. Jim doesn't reply right away. He could just smile and open his arms in a gesture that says you're looking at one, his teeth shining under his great walrus mustache, but that wouldn't be his style, or the style of most cowboys. There is an arrogance, to be sure, but it is a hushed arrogance, something you see when they're at work. It is reflected in their horsemanship, in their expertise with a rope or a branding iron.

"There's so many cowboys from so many different walks of life that it's hard to start picking out qualities. I know good cowboys that never even seen a cow until they was grown men. One thing about being a good cowboy, though, is you've got to have a lot of common sense. You've got to have a lot of patience with animals—that's not necessarily true with people. You don't have to have a lot of patience with people. But you've got to have respect for other people—especially that."

He is quiet for a moment, leafing carefully through his thoughts. "You've got to like the work you do. You've got to be dedicated to it. Because in punching cows there's nothing about money that would attract anybody. I know boys that are punching cows for a lot less than me. But they wouldn't change for nothing in the world. They like being cold and being hungry and wet and dirty and dusty and dry. It just takes a certain kind of man to be a cowboy."

Listening to Jim, I am reminded of something a young hand on the Pitchfork Ranch down in Guthrie, Texas, told me: "This always has been one of the sorriest damn paying ranches in the country. I could go thirty miles down the road and get a hundred dollars more a month." Why, then, did he stay? "Because this is the kind of ranch I was always looking for. It's real honest cowboy work."

Jim brings the pickup to a stop beside a tank we've come out to check. He

Ladder Ranch cowboys

watches water barely dripping from a pipe and swears for a full minute. He grins and says, "You know, you can't work cattle without cussing. There's just no way to ride a bronc horse or work cattle or windmill without cussing. Cattle won't move, they won't go nowhere if you don't cuss them." Presumably the same was true of this, of any aspect of windmilling, one of his least favorite jobs. The tank is nearly empty. He points to a large storage tank on a hill that appears to be at least half a mile to the east. The pipe between here and there has plugged up. He will have to dig up a couple of sections at a time and run his snake through it until he finds the clog.

Driving again, he picks up where he left off. "I've seen fast cowboys and slow cowboys. That don't have anything to do with it. There's a time to be fast and a time to be slow. It's nothing to do with personality. I don't have to like a man, but I can still respect him because he's a good cowboy. I've seen it happen. I mean, in town a man may be the biggest shithead in the world, but when you get him ahorseback and get him out working there's nobody I'd rather be working with or have backing me up."

How do you tell? There are no diplomas. Men do come to a ranch recommended. But such recommendations don't often carry a lot of weight. Every outfit works differently and expects its men to comply. "A feller will hire out and say he's been punching cows everywhere and he can make one little mistake and you can tell exactly how long he's been at it. Usually it's because he don't respect the people he's working with. There's so many rules, so many things that cowboys have to know. There's a whole cowboy book of etiquette that's never been wrote: You don't ride another man's horse. You don't hit another man's horse. You don't even cuss another man's horse for fear that somebody'll hit you in the mouth. You don't ride in front of anybody. Somebody'll rope you and drag you to the earth if you ride in front of him."

Nobody is just born a cowboy. You have to learn it. Maybe it's easier if you've lived around it, maybe not. Most good cowboys agree on a couple of points. You have to want to learn; you learn it from someone you respect. You keep your eyes open and your mouth shut. You don't make a spectacle of yourself at any time. It doesn't hurt to ask questions but you'd better pick your time.

Jim had found a couple of old-timers, men he respected, men who had shown him the ropes. "People would say that if one of them done something, that was the right way to do it. I figured that if I could do it as close to the way they done it as I could it would be right and maybe some day people'd say that about me too.

"There was a man they called Cowboy Jones," he recalls. "Cowboy Jones taught me a lot of stuff. And I worked with another old man on the Bivins Ranch over in Texas named Mr. Lester Byrd. He'd been working for the Bivins people for fifty-five years and he taught me a whole lot. Lester Byrd and Cowboy Jones was both good cowboys—still are—well, Mr. Byrd may be dead now. Hell, he was seventy-five when I was on the Bivins place and that's been eight or ten years ago. Yeah, he's probably not with us any more. He had glasses about that thick"—Jim holds up his finger and thumb, measuring off an inch of air—"and a hearing aid

*Three generations of Chacons, Steve Trigg
Ranch*

plugged in both ears, but he still carried his weight. The only thing I ever seen that that old man couldn't do was lift a hundred-pound sack of cake. But he got ahorseback every day and if you didn't watch him you'd have to call him down about roping cattle. Because he sure would stick his rope on something if it got too close to him. He was quite an old cowpuncher. You'd be coming to the house or going out to a pasture somewhere and he'd show you a trail you'd never seen. I'd been there quite a while myself and he'd say, 'Let me show you something, Jim.' And we'd cut off down this trail and get to where we were going about an hour quicker than we would have if we'd have went my way. And he wasn't one of them old pushy men, either. He was a wonderful old feller."

Sometime in the late afternoon Jim mentions another of a cowboy's major concerns: first-calf heifers. On the Bell, as on a number of ranches with progressive breeding programs, they use longhorn bulls on their heifers. "Progressive" used to describe anything having to do with longhorn cattle has a strange ring. For years cowmen worked to breed the longhorn out of their herds. So successful were they that J. Frank Dobie wrote their epitaph: "The longhorn is of the past—a past so remote and irrevocable that sometimes it seems as if it might never have been, though in years it was only yesterday. It is easy for the ignorant, the superficial and the self-adulating to regard that vanquished dominator of annihilated ranges as a monstrous joke on cattle-kind, a kind of phantasmagoria of vacancy now populated and machine-modernized. But I have an immense respect for the breed."

And so, it seems, do a growing number of ranchers. They have discovered that the success ratio is far greater with the longhorn bulls on their first-calf heifers than with other bulls. "The little calves look like jackrabbits, with them big ears and funny long legs," Jim declares, "but that don't matter. Every calf you get from a heifer is like gravy. Them little longhorn calves is tough and they don't mind being born in a blizzard."

To put it all together and make it work, with mother cows, heifers, bulls, and steers, a cowboy needs to have something called cow sense. This is a quality not unlike the gardener's "green thumb" and almost as difficult to define. "Cow sense is being able to outthink a cow. I used to say people had to be born with it, but I guess that's not true. You can develop cow sense. But you've got to have it, you've got to know what a cow's going to do. There's a time to rush them and a time to be slow. I can go out here by myself and pen a bunch of cows and work them better than if I had three other guys with me who didn't know what they was doing. You've got to know which way a cow's going to run and the shortest way to head her off; you've got to know where she's going to hide her calf. I've got this little place out here where I calve heifers that you'd drive into with your pickup and think, Well, hell, you can see everything in this place from your truck. But there can be six heifers out there having calves and you can drive within fifty foot of them and never see them. You've got to know where that heifer's going to drop her calf. You've got to know which way the cattle are going to go, what they're going to do, how they're going to act, how they're going to react. You've just got to think like a damned cow. I figure I can

Jake Diggs

think about as good as any cow and sometimes they amaze me, just amaze me."

It is almost five when the school bus returns with the Eicke kids. Jason wants to ride a new bronc before supper. He sets a pinch of Copenhagen under his lower lip and then ropes the bronc, a roan with a blaze face. Jim coaches him, offering advice about the new horse. Jason listens, nodding, but he has his own opinions. This makes Jim smile. Obviously, they are friends—in a way that many teenage boys and their fathers never are. Something Jim would attribute to the life.

Jason brings out his saddle. I compliment him on it. Fixing me with an earnest look, he says, "I think it makes everybody look up to a hand if he takes pride in his gear."

Jim agrees. "Yeah, you can tell by looking at a man's rig how good a cow-puncher he is. He may have an old wore out rig but if that sonofabitch's greased and took care of you'll know he's a good hand. He may have the raggedyest old stuff you ever saw but there'll be a silver concho polished up on it or he'll have a pair of silver bits. There's all them little signals to how much a feller knows. Hell, you can watch a man get on a horse and tell just how many horses he's been on."

Months later in this same corral, another young cowboy, Brian Thomas, will ask me to photograph him with his new saddle; it was built in Arizona by Dick Foster and has a look that no factory saddle could ever have. Part of its beauty is contained in Brian's pride. When I mention this incident to Dick Foster in his shop in St. David, Arizona, he says, simply, "They go out with your name on. It's there to tell whoever wants to know that you done the best job you could on it."

Jim turns his concentration to Jason and the horse he's trying to snub to the post in the middle of the pen. Jason, who has his mother's smaller frame and features, displays what Jim most admires in a cowboy: good common sense. He is slow, gentle, and firm; and he's quick when he has to be. Jason has a fragile look until you see him in action; then you realize that his whole body is probably callused and as hard as saddle leather.

Jim lets Jason break all the horses now. He oversees it, of course. But the actual riding of broncs is a job for a younger man.

I ask him if he thinks he'll ever retire. "Not unless they make me," he grins. "Or I just get so crippled I can't work. A feller in this business, a cowpuncher, when he's from fifteen to thirty, he might work on five different ranches a year. He's just like any young man, he's going to go see it all. When you get thirty to thirty-five you've accumulated so damn much stuff with your wife and kids that you can't move no more. So you find a place you kind of like and you stay there. The longer you're there, the more they think of you. Pretty soon you become like one of their old horses. They can't just shoot him or sell him to the dogfood people, so they just kind of keep him around."

The bronc begins fighting the post and Jim starts to get up. He thinks better of it and settles back on his haunches, ready if Jason should need some backing up. "You spend thirty-five or forty years on one of these outfits and that's your home. That's where you want to die. You don't want to go to town and be in one of them nursing homes. The ranch pays them, takes care of them, which is the right thing to do. Take a feller who's given you that much of his life and you can't just turn him out. Hell, he's just like one of these windmills; he's been out there pumping all his life. No, cowboys don't retire. Usually, they die just where they're at."

He pushes back his big hat and considers what he's just said. "Well, I know a few old cowpunchers that have retired. Mainly, it's because of their wives. Them women get to wanting to move to town where it's a little easier to go to the store, where they can be closer to the grandkids, things like that. Most guys, when they get up to retirement age they get a little place of their own. Keep a few horses, a few cattle, some laying chickens. It's hard to quit this kind of life when you've been in it forever. You can't just move to one of them cities and live in an apartment, with everybody looking in your winders and screaming next door. If you been used to working every day, you can't just go sit in a park and spit and whittle all the time. You wouldn't last very long. I couldn't live that way. I don't want to. I ain't going to try it. But I've got a long time to think about that. I hope."

The Texas Panhandle is a big, wide, hard country full of incredible surprises, some as breathtaking as the Palo Duro Canyon which opens up south of Amarillo like a smaller version of the Grand Canyon, and some which possess a more subtle beauty like the Canadian Breaks, and some which are beautiful in an even quieter way like the wild hills along Turkey Creek.

Drivers on Interstate 40 who yawn their way across that ungodly flatland that comes out of Oklahoma, passes through Amarillo, and cuts straight for New Mexico, and who are startled only momentarily by Stanley Marsh's Cadillac Ranch and perhaps left gasping by the sulphurous cloud that hangs over the huge feedlots at Wildorado, have no idea how suddenly the country on either side gives way to these breaks and canyons, how suddenly it can take on a beauty that destroys the bad reputation this rich and uncompromising country has earned.

Stopping a few miles west and south of Clarendon, Texas, on a dirt road carved around a red clay hill overlooking Mulberry Creek, I climb up to look out across a section of the JA, the famous old ranch Charles Goodnight built with the substantial financial backing of a wealthy Irishman named John Adair. It was 1876 when Goodnight moved into the Panhandle. In a series of shrewd and sometimes ruthless moves that seem to have been the accepted procedure of the day, Goodnight took over the entire Palo Duro Canyon, built up a significant herd of cattle, and within the short space of a few years earned Adair a handsome profit. Charles Goodnight was typical of many of the men who made it in the Panhandle, their spirit as raw as the constant wind, their tenacity as stubborn as the ancient, gnarled mesquite.

The Panhandle still breeds cowboys as true to the original model as they come. All over this part of West Texas, men with incredible respect in their voices named cowboys who had been leaving their marks on the cattle business for years and years: Snooks Sparks, Jiggs Mann, Harley Longan, Gerald Martin, Frank Derrick, Tom Blasingame. The list goes on and on. Of them all, all the ones still employed,

Opposite: Jay Frost

4 1

still in the saddle, Tom Blasingame, a cowboy on the JA, has been at it longest.

When you first meet Tom you suspect him of the kind of shyness that has come to be a trademark in cowboys. It is there, in his manner, his bearing, but he opens up, a smile spreading over his whole face. He is generous with his time and obviously loves to talk about the old days. "I started helping cattle buyers in Oklahoma when I was seven or eight years old—maybe ten," he says. "It was about 1907. I had a good little pony. I could ride all day, just the same as a man. They'd hire me and pay me two bits a day to help them drive cattle to market. Didn't have any trailers or nothing back then."

For a variety of reasons Tom remembers the name of one man who gave him steady work during the summer months when he was out of school. "Woody Woodward was his name, a big cattle buyer, and he was just flying all over the country buying up cattle. We'd drive them to where he could ship them. We'd generally get into town about dark. We'd put the cattle in the stockyards and we'd be starved to death. You know how it is when you're a kid growing." He stops and smiles again, showing what remains of his teeth and a fretwork of gold. "Woody was a big tall feller and wore them big heavy spurs. We had plank sidewalks then, wasn't no cement. He'd drag them spurs across them boards and make a big racket. We'd go into a restaurant and he'd say, 'Give me a T-bone steak and bring the kid a bowl of chili.' My feathers fell right there. I was really wanting one of them big T-bones. Them steaks was big, you know—off big steers and dry cows. They'd bring them out on a platter that long." He holds his hands far enough apart to fit a Thanksgiving platter and laughs.

This morning Tom drove up from his own camp to help gather a pasture a couple of miles east of headquarters. At just after 4:00 A.M. when he left his house the sky was clear and still full of stars. By the time he reached headquarters, however, black clouds had boiled up out of the south and east. Then, during breakfast, a drizzle started.

Now, waiting in the dayroom of the sprawling stone bunkhouse to see if the storm will blow over, the young cowboys move in close. Although they pretend to be busy with other things, they are eager to hear what Tom has to say. One is punching holes in a new pair of spur leathers; another opens his knife and picks at the scabs of blood and manure from the previous day's branding and castrating that have dried on his chaps. Tom knows why they've stayed inside. He did the same thing when he was a young man punching his way through New Mexico, Arizona, California, and wherever else his curiosity and wanderlust took him. He would cowboy all day and listen late into the night as the older men sat close to the campfire and spun tales of their adventures.

From the beginning, Tom Blasingame knew he was going to be a cowboy. It was a kind of destiny. I imagine his being obsessed by it, reading the work of early cowboy writers Charlie Siringo, "Teddy Blue" Abbott, and Andy Adams, creating in his mind the image of himself as a cowboy, and refusing to think of anything else.

In those days, being a hand on one of the oldest, biggest, and most famous

Bert Ancell

Below and following pages:
Horse breaking, JA Ranch

spreads in the Texas Panhandle was as fantastic as space travel or testing exotic aircraft is today. Tom would accept nothing less. So in 1916, when he had had enough of day-work for cattle buyers, of driving mules and helping with the hay, and cowboying for smaller outfits around his home in Oklahoma, he set out. He knew exactly where he was headed. "I saddled a big iron gray horse I had, a good horse, one cold February morning and rode into this ranch the next day. Got a job."

For Tom, the secret of it all was right there in that big iron gray gelding. "I just wanted to be on a horse, wanted to be in the saddle. Oh, I liked horses. I guess it was just ingrained in my soul—like a man craving tobacco or whiskey, you know."

This is a statement I hear from ranch to ranch, cowboy to cowboy. It is, finally, the horse that makes the difference. They love to be on a good animal, to feel the swells of the saddle against their thighs, the way the cantle fits their buttocks, the slight stretch and give in the stirrup leathers. Over on the Steve Trigg Ranch just beyond Mosquero Canyon in eastern New Mexico, Leland Earl would be even more adamant in his declaration. "Cowboying's a hard life. The pay's not good. There's no retirement. But I just love to ride horses. I could ride all the time. If something ever happens to my legs I want a seat built on my saddle so I can stay on. I've told my wife that when I die to just put me on a horse and let it go till me and the saddle come off, and then the horse can go free. This is the life I always wanted. I can't even think of another life."

What Tom found on the JA were better horses than he had ever imagined riding. "Them horses they had when I first come here was super horses. I never seen nothing like it. You couldn't get them any better I don't believe. This outfit and the lower Matadors had the best horses I ever saw or ever rode." He talks as if he were describing beautiful women with grace and spirit. "Had Morgan and Steeldust mixed, you know, and a little Spanish too. Had that Spanish blood in them. Makes a good horse. You didn't break them until they was four or five years old. They'd pitch for, oh, maybe six months to a year after you broke them. But after they quit pitching that was it. They would go right on and make good horses. They learned a lot faster than a younger horse. They had more balance to them, more sense, you know."

Every puncher has his opinion, his personal preferences when it comes to a mount. They can be as radically different as the men. Another cowboy from Blasingame's era, an old hand I met at the centennial celebration of the Pitchfork Ranch down in Guthrie, Texas, also liked the JA and its horses but he preferred to drift on and settle at the Matador. "There just wasn't enough romance on most of them ranches. And that's what I wanted, the romance of it. Them Matador horses had more fire in their blood. They wasn't tame like in the other places."

Even in those days when he was wilder and full of his youth, Tom's idea of romance was much different from riding wild horses that might go to pitching any time they took the notion. He liked a good dependable working horse, spunky and smart at the same time. "We had three or four horses in each mount that we used for roundup horses. In action, with a good man on them, they'd make cow horses. We

had lots of cutting to do. We'd go to working cattle about the twentieth of April on this outfit and wind up about the first of December. They didn't wean nothing then. Cows weaned them calves out on the range. Day after day you'd have four or five hundred mother cows in the roundup and you had to cut the yearlings out. That was where you made your cow horses. We'd gather those yearlings, take them to shipping pastures. Had lots of cutting, a world of it."

I ask Tom what he likes best about cowboy life. He cups his hand to his ear and asks me to repeat the question. Then he fixes me with an intense look and his stern reply echoes up into the skylight. "I don't like it too well now," he declares. "But

Below (with cigarette):
Emmitt Faulkner

Right: Stevie Chacon

back then we had a good time. Even if we worked hard we enjoyed it. Country was cleaner. There wasn't no weeds. There was more cattle work, you know—cowboying. This we do nowdays ain't nothing. Not much to it. Little old pastures, pickups and trailers, this-that-and-the-other. Do a lot of chute work. Too much. I don't like it at all. It's altogether different. Didn't dehorn nothing then. Didn't vaccinate or nothing. It was all just clean range work. Course, we done a world of work, lots of cattle work."

He pauses. The young cowboys from the bunkhouse have stopped trying to disguise their interest. They wait, their eyes on Tom. The previous week on another ranch in another state, a young cowboy had voiced his own lament about the changing times. "We could do the same work as they done. Only problem is nobody wants it nowadays. It ain't us; it ain't the cowboys. No place punches cows the way they done years ago. They can't afford to no more."

Tom Blasingame wouldn't hesitate to take exception to the young puncher's opinion. "You know how things change," he says. "Cowboys them days was more alert. Kind of had cow sense. Noticed everything. And they didn't talk so much like they do now. You take a bunch of these fellers at a roundup now and they'll get together and go to jabbering. Used to be you stayed in your place and watched your business and kept your mouth shut. I worked in places where they fired you if you talked too much. You knowed just what you was supposed to do and you done that." After their dressing down the cowboys are no longer looking at Tom; their eyes are focused on the floor or into the distance. But they're still waiting, still listening.

Even if he didn't crave broncs for horses, Tom was possessed by his own romantic streak. He was a young man and a young man liked to move. "When I left here I went to Arizona, to the Double Circles, a big outfit forty-five miles northwest of Tucson on Eagle Creek. They ran fifty thousand mother cows. We never did get through with work, worked year-round. I went from there to the LLLLL up close to Globe and when I left there I went to the Cross Ss on the Apache Reservation."

The words, the names of the ranches, their brands a series of letters and symbols strung together, have a magical ring, a quality that has stayed in Tom's voice for over sixty years. "In Arizona, when I first went there in '18, it was just like I imagine it was around here in 1880 and '90. You camped out the year around—never knew what a house was. Didn't have any houses on them reservations. You set in that tepee in the wintertime and the summer—if it was raining. The Circles was a pack outfit. Didn't have any wagon. Wasn't no roads. You packed your bed and chuck stuff on little mules, just moved around with a pack outfit. It was awful rough country. Rocky. Course I was young and healthy. It didn't bother me a particle. Tough, we got used to stuff like that. Had plenty of wood everywheres. Night came we'd build a fire. We'd build them fires up and get around them, you know, and talk and tell tales until time to go to bed. That's when we done most of *our* talking was around them fires."

One of the young cowboys winces again.

Tom continues, fully aware of his audience. "Them old-timers was still alive and they was interesting to listen to. They'd get to talking about gunfights and things like that and I just set there in a trance. I sure wanted to see a gunfight but I never did get to. Come mighty near seeing one there on the Double Circles. These two guys got all heated up over something and they was all set to shoot it out when another feller jumped between them. He was a friend to both of them. Course they wouldn't shoot then." Reaching back through the years has tickled him and he laughs, repeating that he never did see a gunfight.

The rain is beginning to let up. The foreman comes to the door. Nothing is said, but the cowboys know it is time to go. Tom pushes out of his chair and beats the younger men to the door. He disappears in the light drizzle, buttoning his jacket, and heading for where the horses wait in the pickups and trailers.

The road to Tom Blasingame's camp circles behind the huge main house and the other quarry stone buildings of headquarters, climbs to the highest point on the ranch, and then plunges in a sinuous descent until it finally ends up, miles away, at the edge of the Prairie Dog Town Fork of the Red River. Tom meets me at the door of a house that is beginning to show its age badly. I had been told at headquarters that after Tom was gone they would probably just close up this place, because nobody else would ever want to live down here. It is remote, even from headquarters and

Kelly Shannon (Chad Shannon in corner)

Larry Smith

the other camps; there is no electricity, and almost none of the conveniences most of the camp men's wives demand these days.

When we shake hands I am surprised again that Tom's hand is as hard as a stick and has the power of a man much younger than eighty-five. He asks me to close the screen door tight, a measure he takes to keep out the snakes. Usually the rattlers don't try to come in but the racers do. "They wouldn't hurt a body but they can sure give you a fright, and they're a damned nuisance the way they run through the rooms, especially if they're after a mouse." He keeps cats for that. They stay outside in the summer. He hears them running along the roof, mercilessly clawing mice from the rain gutters before they can reach the drain spout.

Tom rides almost every day, checking his pastures, the cattle, the fences, the windmills, and water tanks, keeping a watchful eye on everything left in his care. He enjoys what's left of real cowboying and he's content to batch in this old camp. Still, no matter how he laments the passing of the old life, there is one thing he does miss down here—a TV. "It's pretty good in the summertime," he conceded, "because then I can get those major league baseball games over my portable radio at night." His eyes begin to sparkle. Baseball is something he likes to talk about almost as much as his memories of the old days—when punching cows was more to his liking. He is a fan, but only of the major leagues. He feels the same about baseball players as he does about cowboys, he has little patience with men who are not at the

Burl Wynn

49

top. He likes the superstars. "I was up till eleven o'clock last night, listening to a game. Then I had to go to bed so I could get up at four this morning. Oh, I sure do like to hear them boys hit them home runs."

This country, miles from everything else on the ranch and rougher than the rest of it, is still tame compared to the Arizona he recalls. That was the wildest country he'd ever seen. "They had lobo wolves there, cinnamon bears, grizzly bears. Had a government hunter out there year-round, killing them bears and lobo wolves. Them wolves, you know, them lobos are cattle killers. They can hamstring grown cattle, cut that hamstring in two, on both hocks, and just go to eating on them." He gives me a questioning look. "You ever seen a lobo?" I never have. Though I've read of lobos, *Canis lupus occidentalis*, the large gray timber wolf, in the sometime romanticized works of Ernest Thompson Seton and the more factual studies by L. D. Mech. "They'll weigh between a hundred and fifty and a hundred and sixty pounds," he says, "and they're awful fierce. They can make a wicked slash with them fangs of theirs. They cut like a butcher knife. And whenever you'd hear them howl at night you could just feel your hair raising up. They've got a wolfish kind of howl. Lonesome. I just love to hear them lobos howl."

I feel privileged sitting in the presence of this great old man. In fact, there have been few moments in my life so rare and fine. Tom Blasingame is a piece of living history, a testament to another time and another life. He went out to find that life, to live it. He came back richer for it, and after more than half a century he has kept enough of it alive to share.

He sits now in a big rocker, his hands clutching the heavy oak arms. He does not rock while he talks. Once in a while, when he pauses for a moment to ruminate and consider what he has said or what he plans to say, he lets the rocker roll forward, almost as if he intends to get up, then he lets it roll back, stop, and he begins to speak again.

"Yes," he says, "that was the wildest country I ever worked in. They was some wild men working there too. The best cowboys I ever saw was working in that country. They could turn them wild, crazy cattle just like a lobo wolf could. I've watched them lobos round up cattle across a deep canyon from me. I'll tell you they'll sure turn when a lobo circles them. I seen a few men over there in Arizona that could turn cattle like that—them big outlaw steers and grown maverick bulls. I don't know how they did it. I never could quite do it. Most of the time they'd split up and go on all sides of me. They had a little fellow there—Arch Brannon was his name—he could turn them just like a lobo wolf and keep them together."

Tom shakes his head and the chair makes another trip forward, the loose flooring under the linoleum creaking. "I don't know what made him different. I guess he was kind of like a major league baseball player, like a Willie Mays or a Mickey Mantle, them superstars. Well, I guess that's the way he was. He just had something nobody else had. Savvy and the know-how—something like that. He just knowed cattle better than most men, knowed what to do better. That's the only way I could figure it out. He could catch them maverick cattle in that brush

Following pages: Gathering and branding, Frying Pan Ranch

country. He had good horses and he could get through that brush smooth and easy." Tom is seeing it again, through eyes narrowed to slits in the half-light of the room. It is a memory he likes, one he's kept in the front of his mind all these years. Arch Brannon was a cowboy he looked up to, a cowboy whose life gave his own life a purpose and a meaning.

"Arch was just like an Indian—wild. He didn't like to stay with nobody. Every winter he stayed off by hisself down in the wildest country I ever saw and gathered and branded them big steers, mavericks. Some fellers he wouldn't mind staying with. Me and him was pretty good partners. A feller named Ike Rude stayed with him one winter. Arch liked Ike all right."

But, in general, Arch Brannon wasn't sociable—even with men he knew. It was a trait that fascinated Tom. He began watching him, taking note. "We'd start out every morning by finding out how we was going to split up and go to work from camp. Arch would stay out to one side or back behind the others. Directly, someone would drop back and want to talk to him. If he didn't want to talk or didn't care for that feller, he'd ride on up toward the lead and get away from him. Men soon caught on not to bother him.

"Everybody liked Arch," Tom says. "He didn't bother anybody, didn't talk about anybody. Once in a while around the fire at night you could ask him something about what happened a long time ago or something. He wouldn't say a word. You'd finally think he wasn't going to answer you. After a while, he'd clear his throat and he'd answer you. He studied a long time before he'd ever answer a question. That's just the way he was. It was natural with him." Now Tom grows silent, a thin smile on his lips. I wonder if he hasn't slipped completely back into that time. Maybe he was hearing the crackle of the hot mesquite and choya fire, the first cries of the lobos testing the night air.

"One time," Tom begins again, "I went to Clifton with Arch. There was a big pool hall there and a saloon, what they called One-Eyed Wiley's Place. It was right on the Frisco River. And there was another old-timer in there—old and cranky. You could tell he was mean—cranky, stove up, and stiff. He knowed Arch and when we got inside he come walking over to meet us. He asked Arch about some feller he didn't like, some feller who'd caused him some trouble." Naturally, this was no way to approach Arch Brannon. "Old Arch he pulled Bull Durham out and started rolling a cigarette, and after he got that cigarette rolled he lit it and took a puff or two and then just kind of looked off like he was looking at the ceiling. He never did answer that feller a word, never did. That feller just finally turned around and walked off. He was wanting to get Arch to say something bad about this other feller. Old Arch wouldn't do that. Meanest thing I ever saw a man do."

While he was on that ranch Tom studied Arch's ways and took from him what he could. There was plenty more he wishes now he'd stayed to learn but he was young then and the itch to move was always with him. "I thought Arch was the best cowboy I ever saw in my life. He was just an expert, that's all there was to it. If I'd have stayed on there and worked with him for several years I imagine I'd been a

better all-around hand. But I wanted to see more country. I went on to different outfits and worked. I wanted to see the range country, the big outfits. I guess I did get quite a bit of experience thataway." His laughter starts. "Didn't lose any anyway."

Tom would never again experience the same kind of work or men he had found in Arizona. Of course, he didn't realize that until he finally ended up in California. "It was altogether different. It was tame. That was in the Imperial Valley and they had gentle cattle. They brought them big steers out of Old Mexico and run them on barley and alfalfa fields that was irrigated out of the Colorado River. They wintered about seventy-five thousand steers in that valley every year, and they paid good wages.

"It was a good place to winter. You had lots of stuff to eat. On the coldest day you'd just barely get a little skim of ice early in the morning and it would warm up in the daytime and melt it. Wonderful winter country, but I couldn't stay there no longer than April. It got too hot for me. It wasn't a healthy heat. It was below sea level and there was something about it that would get you. Them people that stayed there in the summer had bad complexions. They wasn't healthy. And if you had a bad heart it would kill you."

He cleared out of California and started working his way back. Texas ranches had the kind of horses he liked, and there was a significant difference in the food. "If you had a chuckwagon you got a little better cooking. On them pack outfits, water was pretty scarce and some of them cooks was pretty nasty—filthy. And you got burned out on them beans and meat, which was about all you had to eat down there. Texas had better cooks, chuckwagon cooks. There was fellers that wouldn't do nothing else but that. They were just natural-born chuckwagon cooks. Paid them good, you know. But they played out, like everything else. The old ones got too old and nobody else wanted to cook with a pot rack over a fire and that fire smoking and the wind blowing—and the dust. It was a different world altogether."

Tom lets the chair rock forward, the loose board groaning again. This time he pushes himself to his feet. He leads the way outside where he stands looking down toward the river. One of his cats, tired from stalking birds and mice, has fallen asleep in a patch of sun on the roof, his front paws hanging over the edge of the shingles. "I come back here in '34," he says, hooking his thumbs in the band at the top of his chaps. "Got married and been here ever since. I guess it'll be fifty years next year."

Without mentioning the word retirement, I ask Tom how long he thinks he'll continue cowboying. He draws himself up to stand a little straighter. "Well, as long as I've got the strength and energy I've got now there ain't no use of quitting. Not as long as they'll keep me on the payroll. Some of these days they may decide I'm too old and tell me that's it. If they did and I felt like I do now I'd try to go somewhere else and get a job. But I don't know whether anybody'd hire me to cowboy. They might hire a feller as old as I am to be a caretaker around the headquarters, something like that. But I wouldn't want that. If I can't be on a horse, then I'll just call it quits."

Opposite: Denley Norman

I just didn't fit anywhere," Jim Whiteker admits, folding his arms and relaxing against the fender of his pickup. He wears a full-crown brown hat and a black silk wild-rag knotted loosely at his neck. "I was a town kid—from Lake Jackson, Texas."

There was no reason Jim should have become a cowboy. He didn't know a damn thing about it and he didn't dote on it like all those displaced town kids out looking for some different form of escape. For two years he held down a job in Austin, Texas, working on cars. Finally, the heat, the grease, and the annoyance of having a boss pressure him into bringing every job in under the flat rate got to him. He checked out and drifted to Arkansas, doing whatever he could to stay alive. "I got to odd-jobbing, working in the logwoods, working in the hayfields, helping out with their forty head of cows here and their hundred head there." It wasn't long, however, before Jim got his fill of the insecurity of that life, along with the smell of the exhaust from a two-cycle engine and the brittle, headaching whine of the chain saw. However, in the process he stumbled onto the profession he felt he was really cut out for: working with cattle. "It seemed that luck or fate or whatever you want to call it was on my side. I met a boy there in Arkansas who had a brother in Montana that had a ranch. I wrote him a letter and he said, 'Yeah, I need a hand.' So I moved up there and I've been doing it ever since."

Jim is a tall, thin cowboy with square shoulders and long, sinewy muscles. In his narrow, earnest face and clear eyes is reflected the kind of honesty he insists is essential to living the good life, which is the life he wants. During his long slow trip back into the Southwest from Montana, he worked on a number of big and important ranches and gained the experience he needed to take over his present camp on the T4, a ranch that headquarters just off I-40 in Montoya, New Mexico, and stretches for miles northward to and beyond Conchas Lake, where it eventually borders with the Bell Ranch.

The Whitekers' camp sits in a spectacular spot on the top of a large mesa to the

Opposite: Gary Loveland

north of headquarters. I follow Jim up to it, staying far enough behind to watch the dust from his pickup and trailer roll up and funnel off into the wildflowers that line the road. We pass through a herd of twenty-five or thirty deer; they hardly bother to stop feeding long enough to notice the intrusion of our vehicles. After another mile or so, we drop down into a hollow where the house and outbuildings stand among the trees, protected from the worst winds.

Jim coaxes his horses out of the trailer and leads them to water. Something in the tank flashes the sun. I lean close to see what it is. A number of the kind of huge golden carp you see in Japanese gardens blunder slowly through the clouds of algae and moss that hang in the water. They seem unmoved by the presence of the horses.

"Maybe it's a form of claustrophobia," Jim speculates, stroking the neck of the nearest horse, "but I don't much like it indoors. I like to be able to see from here to yonder. I like getting up in the morning and saddling my horse while it's still dark. I like the busy times, the work." He is proud of what he does. What isn't often told about cowboys is that they're usually up and working at four or five in the morning and they may be still going at dark—or all night if it happens to be calving time or there's a sick animal that needs care. If they fall asleep with their boots on, as the myth has it, it's probably not a preference: They were just too worn out to take them off.

"A lot of people get into it for the glamour," Jim smiles. "For instance, up in Colorado I was working with a horse outfit—they run about fifteen hundred head. They brought seventeen of them to me to break. I started in on them, wooling them out, taking it nice and easy. The foreman came out and said, 'Hey, you got

seventeen horses over there looking at you and you've got to have them ready to go in two or three weeks.' So from then on it was just rope them, choke them down, and come up on top. A lot of kids from around there saw me doing that and said, 'Golly, I wonder if I could go to work helping you.' I said sure. But not one of them stuck with it. They sure enough wanted to stomp some broncs. But when it got down to the nitty-gritty—you know, picking yourself up off the ground three times in a row from the same horse—they quit." He likes the irony of it. "I guess a lot of people either have enough sense not to do it or not enough gall. I don't know which. But it sure wasn't as glamorous as it looked."

Jim unsaddles his horse and turns him out with the rest of his string, roan quarter horses whose healthy coats glisten from good feed and care. Back at the truck, he gets on the two-way radio, which is the only communication he has up here, and calls down to headquarters where the school bus has left his children. He tells his daughter to be sure and catch a ride up with her mother who has spent the afternoon shopping in Tucumcari.

What does his family think of his choice of profession?

"As far as my immediate family," he says, speaking of his folks and his in-laws, "I had to go the outcast route for a while." They didn't much like the idea. But Jim felt obliged to do what his conscience told him was right. He felt, too, that it wasn't all that insane. He is certain he has some natural cowboy in his blood and he seriously believes he inherited a bit more. "As far as I know, I had at least one great-uncle who cowboyed. Course, too, I had a great-great-uncle who was a preacher and his four brothers were hung for being horse thieves. So we changed the spelling

of our last name from A-K-E-R to E-K-E-R. That snuffed out a lot of relatives."

In Jim's mind, it's not so important where you grow up. A cowboy can just happen; sometime he just has to be lured into the environment. "I don't think you can raise kids to be cowboys. And you can't raise them not to be cowboys. All you can do is raise them to have respect for other people and do the best they can, do right. My dad worked for Dow Chemical for forty years but I couldn't see me doing it. He finally said, 'If that's what you're going to do, do it.' Mother didn't like it and she still doesn't. She wants me to get a better paying job—better pay and, I guess, better possessions."

But his wife, Victoria, does not hold to those same values. She grew up in Fresno, California, also a city person. She made the trip with Jim, going from state to state, ranch to ranch. Now, like Jim, she looks at this as the only life she wants to lead. "My wife likes it out here. I don't think there's anyplace else she'd want to be. If I ever decided to pack up and move to town," he says seriously, "it would have to be by myself."

Jim started from scratch. He had to learn everything there was to know about being a cowboy—except what he'd seen in the movies, and the movie part was mostly overstatement and decoration. The way he looks at it, all that he lacked in early experience he made up for in ardent desire. He wanted to do it right and he didn't mind asking questions. "If you don't know anything and you're honest about it instead of talking loud and trying to B.S. your way through it, people are more than happy to help you and teach you what you need to know."

And that pretty much coincides with his idea about what it takes to make a good cowboy. "It's the will. A lot of words have been said on this subject but I think it boils down to one thing: a man's self-honor or pride or whatever you want to call it. It seems like the guys who make hands are the ones that were proud of themselves enough to where they wouldn't not do it. It gives them that little extra something."

The work is one thing; where you work is another. In Jim's opinion, which he shares with every cowboy I ever met, the perfect ranch and the perfect boss do not exist. There is something wrong with every ranch, and every boss is merely another human being complete with his own faults. Some have more problems than others and some bosses are worse. You take it as it comes.

What he likes here at the T4 are the horses; they are the best he has ever seen in a career that has included work on ranches with excellent horse programs. But Jim wants to be more than another puncher forked on a great piece of horse flesh; he wants a job with some definite responsibility, something he can do and be proud of.

"I like to think, to use my mind," he says. "Some places, they come and ask your opinion. You know, they ask what would be the best way to gather cattle, what strategy to use. But these places are rare. Some of the ranches I've been on will give a man a country and say: This is it, you run it. The foreman comes through your country once a week or once every other week and more or less informs you of

Opposite:

Top left: Pete Romero

Top right: Ralph Hager

Bottom: Louis Sanders

61

changes in plans, sees how you're doing, and then leaves you alone. It's up to you to figure out how to do it.

"Some places there's a lot of overlapping, more than I personally enjoy. Like winter before last I was out feeding on the east end of this place and they come up and scattered my bulls on the west end without saying a word. I came uncorked. I didn't know how many bulls they had put where or anything. They just come up and did it and then told me about it afterwards. Well I told them how the cow cleaned the calf about that one. They haven't done it since. It seems like a guy's got to blow up and tell them. It gets to be frustrating when you're not in the driver's seat, when you're not at the wheel."

For a man who enjoys breaking horses as much as Jim does, his statement about what his favorite part of ranch work is comes as a surprise. "I like calving heifers," he says, then concedes, "A lot of people look at it as drudgery." To a certain degree, I would agree with those people. I remember cold nights of being out with a first-calf heifer, when it would be below zero with a wind blowing off the snow. There would come a point when you had to pull off your coat, your sweater, and sometimes your shirt, and thrust your arm far enough inside to get hold of the feet and pull each time the anguished creature pushed. None of that bothers Jim. "It just gets back to that self-satisfaction. There is an art to calving heifers; there's a science to it—an art and a science to all of it. There's more thinking involved. A lot of cowboying is more or less being used. You know, they just need a body on a horse. Any fool can do that. But it's not everybody that can tell a heifer's going to spill before she spills."

Because he learned his skills more or less as a cowboy on the move, Jim knows how worthwhile the ideas and information are that travel the cowboy circuit. "The only different ideas these fellows that have been on the same outfit for twenty or thirty years or more are able to get is what a hand will bring when he comes on the crew. Maybe he'll leave them when he leaves and maybe he won't. Usually, if he's any good, somebody will recognize it and take note. Some of these—I guess you could call them migrant workers—transient cowboys see things done a lot of different ways. Moving around, watching, listening, you see how to do something in a different way. Sometimes it's a better way. Sometimes not. It's important to know how to do things, but in this business it's even more important to see how not to do them."

Cowboys universally have expressed their pleasure at being alone. Man after man singles that out as one of the biggest rewards of the work. The solitude is particularly appealing to Jim. But he does have one reservation.

"The one time I worry about being alone," he confesses, "is when I've got a colt and I'm just putting miles on him. I think one of my biggest fears is being hung up in a stirrup or having a horse fall with me and not being found until it's too late. It's always just kind of chewing on the back of my mind. You've got to do it, of course, but you've always got that little scare back in there." He stops, grasps the shank and rowel of one spur in his hand, sort of idly testing how tight it fits the heel

Snooks Sparks

counter of his boot, and then goes on. "But you know, I think that danger, that sense that something could happen, makes it a better job. It's got that added element of excitement."

Gary Green ought to have known better. Even before he starts the pickup, Gary pauses in the steamy, overheated cab to tell me that he'd been warned often enough. "My dad tried to discourage me from being a cowboy, from going into the cattle business—period. He said, 'There's a lot of disappointment in that life and you never make any money at it.' But I didn't listen to him. He was right in many ways. There is a hell of a lot of disappointment for a cowpuncher that makes his life working on these cow outfits. And I like to move around here and there, work on different ones." Which to Gary's way of thinking only seems to compound the

problem. "You get your big bubble—your dream—built up about this new outfit you're going to work for. You've heard all these good things about it. Then you get to working there and it ain't never like you thought it was going to be. There's always something to pop your bubble.

"And he was basically right on the money part of it too. You darn sure don't get rich. But speaking for myself and most of the cowboys I know, I'd say you can make a decent living punching cows. I'll sacrifice the boat and the camper and the big car and everything for being able to live out here in the open and raise my kids where they can be away from all that garbage in town."

Ask cowboys scattered over cow country about established young punchers they have worked with or seen working or maybe only heard about, young men they remember, and Gary Green's name will be on the list. Maybe it's his style. Whatever you call it, there's something just a little different in the way this young cowpuncher does things.

Gary leaves a definite impression, especially seen in profile, with his heavy eyebrows and big, well-groomed mustache. He is a cowboy's cowboy, a perfectionist, a real journeyman in the trade. Guys starting out, buttons they're called here in the Southwest, watch him carefully. For one thing, they are impressed by his equipment, the way he has his saddle just so—built to fit and then modified to go along with the changes in his riding style, his thinking, changes that reflect the work habits of the different places he's worked.

Then there's a big locked box he keeps standing against the wall in one corner of the saddle room here at the Bell Ranch headquarters. "The box," the others call it and they'd like to joke about the box—except they don't really joke about Gary Green. There's something special about him that precludes joking. You see it in the full, uncreased crown of his hat, the gold watch chain, and the little jingle-bob on the shank of each spur, the details. And you have the feeling that a couple of these young punchers have studied the construction of that box pretty closely. One of these days they may turn up on another ranch with one that looks a lot like it.

Gary twists the key in the ignition, the starter grinds, and the engine fires. For a moment it seems uncertain that the thing will keep going. He tromps the foot feed to the floor, clearing out the carburetor. We circle the shop, pass the bunkhouse, the manager's house, and then head up the hill toward the south pastures, where he needs to check and make sure last night's rain didn't wipe out the watergaps in the fences.

In talking about Gary, some of the other cowboys used the word buckaroo. "I used to call myself a buckaroo," he says, slowing for a cattle guard that sends a stiff tremor up through the pickup's ruined suspension. "I don't call myself nothing anymore, just a feller that works for wages on a cow outfit."

However, his time in the Northwest must have had some effect, because when you see him that is what you think: buckaroo. He has that look. And it isn't strictly cosmetic; it goes beyond looks, into the work. "The main difference between cowboys and buckaroos," he explains, "is style. Buckaroos pride themselves in

fancy gear, in having a little more finesse in everything they do—everything from what they wear down to the way they ride and rope. If they were dragging a bunch of calves at a branding, they wouldn't take anything to the fire unless they had both hind feet. It's little things like that that make the difference. Buckaroos are a more independent breed of guy. The sonofaguns, if they don't like it here today, they're gone. Of course they might come back in a month. But it seems like down here in the Southwest there is a certain feeling of—I don't know what you'd call it— dedication to the outfit or something. These guys seem to feel that if they hire onto an outfit they've got to stay there. They kind of set roots in. You see guys on these places who've been here for forty years or more."

Gary never feels obligated to stay on a ranch just because they hired him. He knows his job and does it; he carries his weight. Maybe the urge to move is in his blood, maybe it's curiosity, or maybe it's the nagging desire to find that illusive, perfect ranch. "I think that's part of being a cowboy. You've always got your ears up and your eyes open. There's a couple of outfits I'd still like to work for—Babbits over in Arizona, the Spanish Ranch in Nevada, except I hear they don't pay anything, and the 6666 in Texas."

"I hate pickups," he mutters, double-clutching in an attempt to hit third gear. "I hate pickups in general, but this sorry damn piece of tin tops the list. It'll make you glad to ride the worst horse on the place." The transmission grinds for a second, then pops in with a lurch.

Ask Gary who influenced him most when he was starting out and he can answer in a single word. "Granddad. He was the basic reason I wanted to be a cowboy. He was always just exactly what I wanted to be. He knew horses and cattle. He'd been to the old school. He was the kind of guy, and most of them old boys were, who wouldn't go out to do a job if he couldn't do it right. He had to do everything right and take pride in it."

No matter how much he revered his granddad, Gary couldn't stay with the old man forever. There came a day when he had to strike out on his own. "I went to Montana and worked for an outfit up there on the Yellowstone River a few miles out of Terry. I worked for one hardass, I'll guarantee you. I mean he tried to kill me."

Gary drives for a while, silent, slowing to study some cattle. This is the best kind of cow country. It is open and clean. It hasn't been overstocked or overgrazed and even in a year as dry as this one the cattle have come through sleek and fat. "That was good for me, though," he says. "When I was growing up I usually just worked with my granddad. And when I got away from home and went to work for this old boy I discovered exactly how tough it could be out in the cold, cruel world. I had to whip and spur. And I guarantee you I was treated like dirt."

Even that wasn't the worst. He ran onto a couple of other ranch managers up north who came right out and said they were not the least bit interested in hiring cowboys to work their cattle. "They claimed that all cowboys were good for was tearing up pickups and sitting around the bunkhouse trying to look like Charlie Russell. What they hired were general ranch hands, somebody they could take out

Opposite: Floyd Sanders

Right and following pages:
Colt branding, Bell Ranch

and put on some old gentle horse and tell him how and when to move and then take him back to the house and put him to work hauling garbage or something." Those were tough comedowns for a man with any pride, and pride is a big commodity in a buckaroo, or a puncher of any description.

Since the beginning of the breed, or at least since it began receiving a flood of publicity and praise starting sometime in the last century, cowboy life has become a catchall for almost every kind of romantic who could struggle into a pair of boots and a big hat and throw his leg over a horse. Although Gary understands the impulse, he still feels these people ought to stay in town and forget about it. But he won't deny that cowboys, bona fide cowboys, are romantics in their own right. "A cowboy can make his life as romantic as he wants it. And I think that's one of the reasons cowboys are so traditional. They take pride in and enjoy doing things the old way, whether it's tough on them or not. The old-timers might not have had any better way to do it. But a lot of today's cowboys just enjoy doing it the old way because that was the way the old-timers did it. And as far as being romantic I don't think there's anything more romantic than being around Mother Nature. I enjoy being out in it, working with horses and cattle."

He guns the pickup through an arroyo still muddy from last night's rain. It shudders up the other side, the wheels spinning and the tired shocks hammering under the fenders, and bangs along the rocky hillside to where Gary can check the fence that crosses it, to make sure the watergap hasn't been hit by a sudden flood of mud and debris and washed out.

"I've known guys that just hated cows," he continues, turning the truck back

to the road. "I mean sure, everybody gets mad at cows now and again. They can be ignorant critters. But I've rode with guys that could not stand to be around cows. Everytime they were, they'd be mad. That would be like me trying to drive a dozer. I can't stand heavy equipment. I just hate it. I don't like the noise; I don't like the heat; I just hate it. So I don't do it. And if a cowboy doesn't enjoy punching cows then he better get out of the business. A lot of times you run into fellers that are out here to look like a cowboy, but they really don't take an interest in what they're doing. I think if you're going to make a good cowpuncher you've got to realize you're there to work cattle. If you don't you're just walking backwards."

Gary swings the truck up onto a grassy spot to go around a piece of road that the rain has gouged into deep, impassable ruts. The front end sinks to the axle and comes to a stop, throwing us both against the dash. Gary tries to rock the thing out, but the damp red clay under the grass turns to grease and the tires only dig in deeper. The four-wheel drive went out months ago and the humongous winch bolted onto the front bumper, added to the weight of the engine, is like a sinker. Gary looks at me and repeats his earlier statement about pickups, about this one in particular.

For the next hour, digging with a shovel and struggling to keep the shaky handyman jack upright, we raise each of the four mired wheels and fill the space under them with rocks lugged down from the nearby hillside. Gary spins the wheels until the tires smoke. This drives the stones deeper into the mud, leaving the truck more stuck than ever. The winch could probably pull us out but in this part of the ranch there is neither tree nor stone big enough or close enough to tie onto with

70

the cable. Finally, Gary shuts off the engine, gets out, and slams the door.

Eventually someone will come looking for us. We have a choice: We can wait here or start walking. It may be evening before the rest of the cowboys realize we are stranded. So it might be a long wait. "We might as well walk," Gary decides.

It is ten miles back to headquarters and the high desert sun burns down fiercely, sending up caloric waves that leave the horizon awash with shimmering mirages.

"If we'd have been ahorseback," Gary says, making an example of it, "this wouldn't have happened."

Gary's spurs snag the grass and short brush and the rowels ring as they drag over the small stones. To keep our minds off the distance, the intense heat, and our growing thirst, we continue to talk. I want to know how you learn. "You keep your eyes and ears open and your mouth shut. The thing that makes the best cowboy is experience. You learn from your peers."

It is a process that apparently never stops. At seventy-five, Walter Ramsey, on the Guadalupe Canyon Ranch in Arizona, can attest to that: "I don't believe a day goes by when you're punching cows that you don't learn something new. It's sure not a dull job."

Gary understands what Walter means. "Whenever I go to a new country I find that the basics are the same but they do a lot of things different. A lot of times I see fellers of the opinion that their way is the only way to work. They might be right and they might be wrong. They might have been raised on some little outfit and never got ten miles from home so they don't know. There might be a feller a few miles away running the exact same type operation in a different way and getting along a lot better.

"In my book, there's two ways a cowpuncher can learn: You can move around and see how things are done on different places by different people or you can stay on one place and learn from the people that come there. You're darn sure not born with that knowledge. And it's not something you can study on at night."

Traditionally, cowboys have not been noted walkers. It is one reason their boots are built with pegged steel shanks and high, underslung heels; they work much better in the stirrup than on the ground. Gary is beginning to feel the strain. He stops and presses his palms against the small of his back. "I guess we aren't in any hurry," he says and stretches out on the ground to rest.

I'm not really pitching questions anymore. There seem to be some things Gary's had on his mind for a long time that he wants to say. "One thing bothers me about the way people think about cowboys." He pulls a grass stem from a clump and chews on it thoughtfully. "And a lot of ranch managers are the same, they get my goat when they harp on this. They have the idea that because a cowboy wants to be out there on horseback, he thinks he's too good to do anything else. But don't let anybody fool you, if you stay on horseback for six or eight or ten hours a day and you're covering a lot of country, that's pretty tough work. Them old horses, they're not rocking chairs."

He is not implying that he doesn't like horses. "No, one of my favorite parts of working on cow outfits is having good horses, young horses you can teach and watch learn." He pushes himself up onto one elbow. "I've broke quite a few colts. It's slowing down a little bit, though. In the last few years I've noticed I just feel every bump and bruise and knock I get. Your age catches up with you pretty fast with those broncs."

When we start walking again, Gary pauses, reaches down—almost, it seems, reluctantly—and removes his spurs. He buckles the two ornately stamped leathers together and slings them across his shoulders. It is the first time in three days that I've seen him without his spurs.

After another couple of miles, we see a windmill in a draw, a tank of steely water glinting in the sun. This has nothing to do with the way the heat tricks your eyes and mind. Gary remarks that unfortunately this's the worst water on the ranch—but it will be wet. There is no way this water can be drunk. Standing in the stock tank it has become hot enough to brew tea. Gary climbs the mill and tries to turn the blades of the big Aeromotor pump. It is too stiff. Miraculously, as he is climbing down, a breeze comes up. The windmill groans; a trickle of water starts out of the pipe. A few seconds later, it is cool enough to drink, bitter, and it is wet enough to get us back on our feet.

Less than two miles from headquarters, we see a cloud of dust boiling up

behind the foreman's white pickup. Gary stops walking; it is pointless to go any farther. We have been discussing the pros and cons of big ranches owned by various corporations. It is a subject he views with mixed emotions. And while we wait, he continues, "I do not like to work for the owners of a ranch. The best job you can have is working for a manager who has been in your boots at one time. One thing about a big outfit is they're going to be able to pay you good money, buy good equipment, and try to do things right. I'm just as much against big business in the cattle industry as anybody because they're choking the family man out, the little guy that's got three hundred head and is trying to make a living off them. But looking at it from my standpoint, where I'm working for wages and never will be able to buy a ranch of my own, this is the place for me, a big operation. And if it's owned by a big corporation, then that's the way it'll have to be. I've got it better than if I had my own place. If we have a big blizzard and lose a lot of cattle, I'm still going to get my paycheck at the end of the month."

It is one of those weird West Texas days that make even the natives a little uneasy. The hot, moist air hanging close to the earth clings to your skin and makes you uncommonly aware of everything you do, even breathing. The sky, faded now to the color of concrete, is a shell of flat, characterless clouds that brood and somehow threaten rain, though the conditions all seem wrong for rain. Tornado is probably

the word in most minds; there is that edgy feeling of something building, something imminent and dangerous.

At the end of a long, perfectly straight, fenced dirt lane the tracks make an abrupt left turn into the camp where Robbie Seale lives. Like most of these places I have visited, the house has a slightly forlorn look, the look of rented houses in an industrial city—comfortable enough but showing signs of neglect, needing small repairs and paint. A broken cow's skull with dark horns hangs askew above the white wooden gate into the yard.

Robbie's wife, Teri, stands on the grass watching two young children play under the skeletal branches of a dead fruit tree. She is small, almost frail looking, and seems hardly old enough to be their mother. She pushes away a number of dogs and cats that surround me, and apologizes. They have them, especially the cats, in hopes they will keep away the snakes. She lives with the constant fear that one of the children will suddenly stumble onto a big rattler that has crawled in from the pastures or come out from under the foundation of one of the outbuildings to find a patch of sun. Many times in her mind she has probably seen herself having to drive the twenty or thirty miles of dirt roads to the nearest doctor. Later, when she stands with Robbie and the kids for photographs, there is a wistful prettiness to her face and another, less easily identifiable quality that might have a lot to say about the strain and loneliness of this kind of life.

Robbie greets me on the porch and suggests that we go to the kitchen where it is a little cooler. He fixes two large plastic glasses of Coca-Cola and we sit at the chrome table. The previous times I've seen him he spoke little more than a polite greeting. So he surprises me as much with his willingness to talk as with his open and direct manner.

Robbie grew up, he volunteers, at Boy's Ranch, the orphanage out on that desolate stretch of highway between Amarillo and Dalhart. This was sometime before or after he lived in Los Angeles, California, and Las Vegas, Nevada; the way he tells the story it doesn't seem to matter which came first. He says it largely to establish what he considers an important fact: Cities and all they represent rank high among the things he hates. What little family he has are all living in cities or towns. Unlike Jim Whiteker, Robbie can't trace his roots to a distant relative who either cowboyed or stole horses. Cowboy was just always in his mind, an image formed in there that he had to complete in real life.

It isn't difficult to see Robbie Seale as a little kid dressed up for the part he wants to play, with toy guns and any of the other cowboy garb he could muster. And I can also see him later at Boy's Ranch. I can see that place, situated on a bleak hill off to the right of Farm Road 1061, and the mark it left on him. He would be pretty much as he is now—only smaller, thinner. Serious, with the same concerned wrinkle to his brow, as if he is bitter about being there—or perhaps only puzzled. His ginger-colored hair would be cropped as close as it is today, in a cut we used to call a burr. Only then he would still have the end of his right thumb, which he must have lost to a rope or some piece of the machinery it takes to run cattle. On an earlier afternoon, when I'd first asked to photograph Robbie and his family, Teri told me that a painter had done a watercolor that looked just exactly like him except the man had painted in the thumb. It made her laugh.

When you are first around Robbie Seale, you get the impression that he's shutting out certain things—and it must have seemed so then, something that might have caused workers at the orphanage and, later, teachers to express their concern   until you realize that under all the close-mouthed silence Robbie is like a thirsty sponge, trying to take it all in, to soak it up, process it, and save it for another time. And he likes to be left by himself to do it.

"Even out there at Boy's Ranch around all those kids," he recalls, "I might have had two or three friends—but that was it. I didn't have anything to do with anybody else." This trait is no less enigmatic to him than it is to anyone else. "I don't know why I'm like that but that's the way I am. I don't care that much about being around people. I'm by myself a lot. I'm not real crazy about crowds. I just like being outdoors. I like animals. I like peace and quiet. I like to be with myself a lot."

This particular day has been unsettling for Robbie and perhaps that explains in part, at least, why he wants to talk. For some time he has been having trouble with a pain in his hips. Finally, this morning, he drove in to have a checkup. The doctor's diagnosis was arthritis. "He told me you need to stay off horses for a month. And try these pills, and if these pills don't work I'd suggest you start looking for another way of going at it, another way of living." Robbie pauses, his mouth set, his eyes narrowed and hard. "No way. I'll just go on like I am. If I have to hurt then I'll hurt. There's no other way for me."

Robbie sits straight in the chair, his spine not touching the back. This could be from the painful ache in his hips or just the way he is, the way he's always been. In addition to his regular cowboy clothes, he wears wide suspenders, the kind I remember were always called braces and are associated in my mind more with firemen than with cowboys. He takes hold of them with both hands and is silent for a few seconds.

While the doctor's findings obviously depressed him, they have, finally, only served to spark his fierce determination. The line of his mouth is more finely drawn than ever. "I want my kids to grow up out here. I've got that boy out there—" He nods toward a window through which the children can be seen playing on the grass between the house and the fence. The boy is small and blond and wears the falling-down pants of a kid still in diapers. "He may not be interested in this kind of life, and if he's not that's fine, but I'd like it to be here if he wants it." In Robbie's eyes, living on a ranch, a little bit isolated, insulated from a world that's fallen apart, has definite advantages. "It seems like to me that today the morals and everything is wrong. If you're raised like this, in the old way, the way it used to be a long time ago—" he begins and then his voice trails off. He ends up by merely shaking his head. "I wish I'd lived in Snooks Sparks and Tom Blasingame's era. They lived in good times. This cow business nowadays, it's okay in some places but it's getting too modern and they've got too many gimmicks. It's just no good. Like branding around here with a butane burner when we've got all this mesquite."

Is it the smell he objects to? "No, it's the noise. You can't hear yourself think. I guess I just like the way people done it in Snooks and Blasingame's days. When I'm their age, they ain't no telling what this's going to be like."

Like Gary Green and Jim Whiteker, Robbie Seale has put in time on ranches all across cattle country. In each of their cases it finally seems to be anything but a footloose, nervous, and purposeless drifting from place to place. Gary Green is perfecting the art, perhaps even trying to keep it pure, trying to find that one bubble that won't pop. Jim Whiteker is looking for a place where he'll be left alone to make most of the decisions about his own work and his piece of country, where he can calve his heifers in peace and quiet. Robbie Seale's ambitions are bigger and unexpected. He is preparing for the day when he can actually take the reins of one of these big cow outfits. "What I hope to do," he says, watching my face to measure the reaction, "is run a ranch. I've seen a lot of country and seen a lot of different ways of going about it. So I'm kind of putting together what I think's the best way."

Robbie's in no particular hurry. In his mind, everything has its own time. In fact, it almost seems that his life is rehearsed. From the start, cowboy was something so deeply rooted in his soul he could never be anything else. He started young and he has kept cutting the facets of experience into his life the way a jeweler cuts a stone. His plan is that carefully thought out, that calculated. He knows how

Opposite top: Terry Pilley

Opposite bottom: Royce Griggs

Dick Foster, saddlemaker

long it's going to take, how long he's going to have to wait to get control of a ranch and do it right. He remembers the bad places and the good places; he learned from both. They are part of the catalogue, the compendium of useful knowledge that he's privately assembling. "I've worked in Nebraska, Arizona, New Mexico, Montana, and Texas," he says. "The place I liked best was Nebraska. I worked on the North Platte River for the Rush Creek Land and Livestock Company. I stayed there six months, which was about the longest I wanted to stay in one spot in them days." And there was a practical reason for his staying on that long. "I liked the way they

Bo Cribbs

operated. They were organized. When you got ready to do something you weren't running around trying to find something to do it with. It was there. And in working order."

Chances are, Robbie got his first look at the cold, cruel world at a much younger age than Gary Green, possibly when he was living at Boy's Ranch. But his first experiences as a cowboy were no easier. "The way I learned was by getting snapped at. That'll stay with you. I've worked for some guys that was younger than I am, but I'd rather work for a man a lot older, one that's been there, one who was down where I am now and has worked his way up through the ranks. Them's the people that I watch and listen to. I've learned more from Snooks Sparks than I have from anybody."

Snooks Sparks. His is one of the names that one keeps hearing in the Panhandle. "You don't have to ask him questions. You just watch him. But he's the type of guy who if you want to ask him something he'll answer you, regardless of how dumb it may sound. I believe in asking questions. If I don't understand something I ask him and he'll explain. I might be coming up against the same situation one of these days and I'll know how to deal with it.

"I've been here for four years, the longest I've ever stayed in one spot. And being around Snooks has been like going to college. He's seen just about everything there is. He knows how to work a man, because he knows how he was worked."

Coming from Robbie, these are high marks. Snooks has shown him a whole new set of standards by which to gauge his own progress as a potential cowboy boss. "I feel that in this business if you can become a foreman then you've gone about as far as you can. You went to the top of your profession. I'm not so sure I'm ready yet. I need to tag along a little more."

Robbie Seale is neither a hopeless romantic nor is he an unreasonable idealist. But one thing he just can't get out of his head is the frightening spectre of the

contemporary cowboy. And to his way of thinking, the changes that have come into the life are nothing to what threatens to change it even further. He likes the job and all of the work that goes with it; he would just sooner be able to do it in better times. "I'd like to live back in the wagon days," he repeats, rattling the glass of ice in his hands. "Everybody's going to oil and gas, poking holes in the ground. You've got to ride around a pipe or a pump to turn a cow. I don't like that. If it gets too bad I'll go somewhere where they're still at least trying to do it like they've always done it."

In spite of his longing for these earlier and, he believes, better days, Robbie's ideas about how a cowboy ought to perform fit all the problems he might face in running a modern ranch. His thinking along these lines is likely the result of his desire eventually to become a foreman. "A good cowboy works his trade," he states firmly. "Too many guys coming up now just want to ride a horse. They don't want to fix a windmill, they don't want to mend any fence. To me they're just playing a role, not working a trade."

Robbie believes that the cowboy who doesn't know the one fundamental rule about punching cows has no place on a ranch, and certainly won't find work on the spread he expects to run someday. "You hire out to take care of cattle. If cattle's out of water because the windmill's broke down, you've got to fix it to get them their

water." Robbie's eyes flash as he drives home this, his first and primary rule. "A lot of people think they're too good to fix a windmill because that's not what a cowboy does. Well, I don't know what their idea of a cowboy is. I think it's somebody who'll do the dirty work just as good as he'll do the nicer part of it. If you're crossing a cattle guard and you see it needs cleaning out then you've got to do it. There's some that won't. They'll quit if you tell them too—especially if they're single. They're in it for the novelty, just playing a role."

Robbie is silent for a moment. From somewhere in the house I hear the ticking of a clock. "That's just my opinion," he adds, flattening his hands on the edge of the table, finished, and ready to get up. "It's not worth much."

On the map, the Geronimo Trail is a broken gray line running east out of Douglas, Arizona. Just past the high school on East 15th Street the shelly pavement peters out and the car begins to float on the loose gravel. The setting sun flashes red and hard in the rearview mirror and out before me, rising from behind the hills, the full moon is the color of a large silver coin. The south wind, which in the fall of the year seems to blow with the single purpose of freighting huge skeletal tumbleweeds and rusty adobe dust across from Mexico, keeps blowing me over into the lefthand lane. Tumbleweeds half the size of a horse come rolling up the roadbed, crash into the car doors, and shatter with an unnerving crunch.

Somewhere beyond the entrance to the Slaughter Ranch, a gigantic land grant that once stretched deep into Sonora and now stands as a much smaller tribute to those times, its holding diminished, its house a national landmark, the road splits and the right fork veers off toward Guadalupe Canyon.

Immediately the road is much rougher; and in the next few miles its condition grows worse and worse. The culverts disappear. I shift down into four-wheel drive to cross streams swollen from the rains of the past week. The road crosses into New Mexico, dips through more rocky streams, and worms its way among the dark trees. In a small clear spot a monument lies on its side. The part of the plaque still visible declares that the Mormon Battalion passed here. The date is obscured by grass. Across a cattle guard, down a steep embankment, then up the other side, and suddenly the car lights flash on three huge white Brahma bulls standing stone still in the center of the road. I might honk at a Hereford or an Angus, but remembering the advice of an old cowboy who said, "If you see them Brahmers turn and look at you it's best to sit your horse a while," I ease out in the grass to go around them. Two miles farther, beyond power lines, beyond phone lines, and beyond any sign of improved roads, I roll into the yard of the Guadalupe Canyon Ranch.

Inside the main house, which these days belongs to the poet Drummond Hadley, Walter Ramsey, seventy-five, hunkers close to the fireplace, holding his hands out toward the flames as if to funnel the heat into the rest of his bones. He has dressed in new Levi's and a new red and white plaid cotton shirt with pearl snaps. His Paul Bond boots were benchmade fourteen years ago. The black French calf vamps could almost be new and the red tops, which are shorter than any I have

Opposite: Sam McDonald and Leo Turner

seen in years, are filled with a complicated pattern of fancy stitching. They have incredibly high stirrup heels, which Walter admits are not so easy to walk on anymore. "Course," he says, a flash of a smile in his eyes, "they wasn't never meant to be walked on that much."

One of Walter's earliest memories is of coming to this house. He was four years old when he first saw it. "Best I can remember," Walter cocks his head to figure his way back through the years, "it was about Eastertime. We came to a friend's house down the canyon for Easter and they was having this dance up here. We all got in the wagon and came up to the dance. An old feller by the name of Hudspath owned this place then. My uncle Vance McDonald bought it later. After he moved in here my dad bought the lower end of the place, which was over in Arizona."

There are other memories of those times, of being a kid in these mountains and growing up with the kind of loneliness that kept families close and gave a strong meaning to work. Sometimes Walter is not clear about the year but always the experience is intact. There was, for instance, the time his dad came home with Walter's first horse. "I guess it was about the end of old Pancho Villa's revolution, somewhere in there. Someone came into Agua Prieta with a whole bunch of old mares and horses to sell. My dad happened to be over there at the time and there was a little old horse in the bunch that he bought and brought home for me. He called him Old Rondo, I don't know why. He wasn't over three years old. He was broke but he wasn't no cow horse. He didn't know anything any more than just to let you ride him. He was just a little Mexican pony."

That was the pony Walter rode up from his dad's ranch to the one-room schoolhouse that sat a couple of miles down the canyon from where we now sit. He went there until the eighth grade. Then, as was customary for kids of the ranches in this area, he moved in to Douglas to board and attend high school. He lasted a week. He was fourteen then. He rode home, told them what he'd done, and got his first full-time job on a neighboring ranch.

Given the upbringing he had and his character, it was almost inevitable that Walter would choose cowboying as the life to follow. But there is something different in the way he describes it, almost as though it were the object of a romance. "From a little old kid up that's just what I had in mind. I don't know why, for some reason I just fell for it."

Through the years, Walter worked in a lot of different kinds of country, but he always preferred the rougher ranches where there was a little more of what he likes to call "real cowboying." "I liked the mountains because ordinarily that was where we got to run the wild cattle. There was more excitement than on those flatter places. I guess in other words I just wanted to be kind of wild and run something wild."

He smokes thoughtfully, watching the fire, then sits back in his chair. "Ordinarily of a morning there would be bucking horses. This one getting bucked off, that one in some kind of storm. Two or three men'd be running after that horse to try and catch him. Wild things such as that. There was never nothing dull about the work."

Even with the wrecks, the wildness, and the unpredictable nature of everything in his daily life, Walter wasn't satisfied just spending all his time on the ranch. "When I was real young I always wanted to be a bronc rider. And I follered that for a good many years. I enjoyed it until I finally got to getting bucked off and crippled up and banged up so bad I finally just had to quit."

Maybe it wouldn't be like that today; rodeo now doesn't hold the same excitement for Walter that it did in the old days. "Nowadays these boys come out on these bucking horses and if they stay up there eight seconds that whistle blows and they pick them off," he says disdainfully. "Back in those days you wasn't even inside no arena. They'd just have cars lined up fairly close together on the sides and that's all the fence there was. When you come out on one of them old broncs you rode him until he quit or you got bucked off. There wasn't nobody there to pick you up after eight seconds."

Like Tom Blasingame and many of the other old-time cowpunchers, Walter laments the passing of a lot of the life. He understands why much of it had to go but he still regrets it. Among the things he misses most are the big stout Steeldust horses they used to ride. He loved amazing those horses, admired them for their

stamina, and believes there is a great deal to be said in favor of the way they were broken. "In them days we didn't fool with a bronc until he was past a two-year-old, coming three anyway. Of course they was wild; they grew up out on the range. The first thing after we'd gathered them was to put a hackamore on them and stake them to a log out in an open place and just leave them overnight on that stake log. It was heavy enough that they couldn't run off with it but it'd still move. Like if they got spooked and run on that rope that log would give enough to where it wasn't apt to cripple them or break their neck or anything like that. They'd get theirselves all tangled up in that rope and fight it a bit but they'd eventually learn not to never run on it after they'd been jerked around by it and throwed theirselves on the ground a time or two. They'd get astraddle of that rope and have that log out between their hind legs and under their tail and they'd soon quit pulling on it. They'd learn to give slack and get out of that rope."

It is evident in the way Walter tells it that he enjoyed snubbing down a bronc, tying him to the log, and then jumping back and watching the creature discover the resistance and go to work on itself. Naturally, that log didn't iron out all of the kinks and wrinkles but it usually saved a man some bad battering. "After they'd been staked overnight we'd take them to the corral the next day and kind of what we called blanket them out. You'd put your saddle blanket on them and go to fooling with them, petting them, putting your saddle on both sides of them. Then you'd put the saddle on them. After you fooled with them for a while with the saddle, you'd get on them and maybe ride them for twenty or thirty minutes. Sometimes they'd blow up and you'd have to ride them until you'd got all the vinegar out of them. Then you'd get down and unsaddle them and maybe feed them. If they still didn't act too good you'd take them back and tie them to this log again. They'd learn more being staked out on that log than you could learn them in six months. Course it's altogether different now. You don't talk to somebody today about staking one of their horses out on a log at night. No way. They're afraid you'd knock a little skin or hair off of them."

Every young puncher I've seen in the past year would give a great deal to be in this room tonight. I have the same feeling I've had over and over during this long odyssey, that time has relaxed its intricate webbing and let me slide from the present. There is, for instance, nothing much here to indicate that we are not sitting before a fire on an evening during Walter's younger days. With the generator no longer grinding away out beyond the bunkhouse, there is no electricity for lights. The fire, which has its own voice, sends orange light flickering onto furniture that could easily fit into another era. I have the distinct sense that if I listen closely I will hear, somewhere out there in the dark, one of Walter's bad broncs fighting the log, the rope singing through the grass, snapping taut, and the horse being brought crashing to the ground with a hollow thud.

"Usually," Walter continues, "we'd ride them two or three saddles in the corral and then we'd take them outside. One or two cowboys'd go with you on gentle horses for the first time or two so if your bronc bucked with you or he broke and run

Opposite: Jesus Perilla

or anything like that they could haze him out from under a low-hanging tree or a fence."

People have different definitions about what is meant by a broke horse. The Diamond A, where Walter worked for a while, figured a horse was broke after ten saddles, which is ten times of being saddled and ridden. Walter didn't agree then, and he doesn't now. "Ten saddles just gentles him enough so he knows he's been rode, but he'll still buck with you. I'd say it takes at least a year, and some of them take more. Some of them at the end of a year's work they're pretty gentle and pretty safe and others at the end of two years you've still got to watch.

"The best thing to do on a bronc horse, at least this's the way we did it then, is to try and do everything on him right from the start that you figure you'd ever want to do on him in a lifetime. Get him tangled up in a rope, drag cattle on him, anything. We used to start roping off our broncs after five or six saddles. And we always used hobbles and learned them to travel with hobbles on. That way if you ever had to lay out overnight or anything you wouldn't wake up the next morning and find out that your horse had gone clear out of the country. Anyhow, that's the way we broke horses in them days."

Ask Walter his least favorite job and he is quick with the answer. "I never cared for riding day-herd. These was them big steers and cows that was going to be shipped when we got to the railroad or the shipping point. Somebody had to go with that day-herd every day the wagon moved. You had to take this herd to where the wagon would be that night. I didn't like that because all you could do was poke along. You couldn't crowd them or anything because they had to graze through the day. It was just a slow monotonous job."

However, there was nothing monotonous about most of the jobs a cowboy did. A man more or less knew what he had to do each day; how it was all to be accomplished was another matter altogether. The work was unpredictable and sometimes it seemed the hardships, the hazards, and the savage tests of physical strength that went with it would never stop. No roundup, branding, or breaking of a bronc was ever exactly the same. They each had their flukes, their little idiosyncrasies and differences that made them somehow unique. But there is in Walter's memory one month that stands out, one month from a long life of hard work and long hours, of standing toe to toe with the elements, one month that was monumental. It was a cattle drive, almost classic in its proportions, a big drive Walter made in Mexico in 1933. He and another man had gone partners in a little bunch of cattle they were running in the Tigre Mountains near Baserac, which lies about seventy-five miles due south of Agua Prieta in the state of Sonora. Walter's uncle had leased a big ranch south of Cananea, a hundred miles to the west, and wanted them to bring their cattle over there.

"It was a miserable trip," Walter begins, but his eyes glisten more from the thrill he remembers than from anything that suggests physical pain. "We started rounding up what cows we had in the latter part of January and we were going to go across the country with them. We left with the herd on the first day of February and

started off that Tigre Mountain just south of the old Tigre Mine. They was a high bluff on the west side of that mountain that ran for several miles. Until the previous summer there hadn't been no way to get off it or get up it. But that summer some boys had figured they could blaze a trail up through a rock slide and take their cattle up that way. That slide was just a break in the bluff and it looked so full of boulders that a wild cat couldn't have gone through it. Well, they went up it afoot, working a trail, just zigzagging up through there to the top.

"By nightfall we got our cattle to the place where they'd worked this trail. It was raining and blowing and we stayed in an old cabin that was there. It had a kind of old zacawiesta roof that kept us dry for part of the night."

Walter takes a stick from the woodbox and pokes at the logs in the fire. Satisfied that they will catch and burn, he slides back into his chair, his hand still fisted around the stick.

The next morning it was still raining and cold, none of which made the cattle any easier to move. "Right at the start of that zigzag trail," he says, tracing it out on the hearth with the stick, "was a kind of jump-off. It wasn't exactly straight up and down but almost. We was having lots of trouble getting anything to go off there. Finally we got the cattle started. Then they had to go because they couldn't turn around or go out on either side. We didn't have to pay no attention to them. We went to trying to put our horses and pack mules off a there.

"One little old pack mule was kind of ornery. She started down through there and some way her feet slipped or something and she went end over end. It was real steep there in the beginning and she must have rolled as far as from here to the bunkhouse, fifty yards. We figured she'd be broke all to pieces, killed or something,

and if she wasn't we'd have to shoot her and get her out of her misery.

"When we got down to her, she'd rolled up into some boulders and couldn't get up. We put a rope around her neck and pulled her out. She got to her feet and there wasn't anything much wrong with her. All that bouncing and rolling'd only knocked a lot of hide and hair off her. The pack was scattered from where she'd started all the way down. We gathered up what we could find of our camp outfit, put the pack back on her, and got on down through the rock slide.

"There was good feed there on the mountainside where we come out of the rocks, so we turned our cattle loose and went off to an Indian cave a quarter of a mile away. We got in that to keep dry. It rained off and on throughout the night and got more constant by morning. We had another high ridge to go over on them Tigre Mountains and by eleven o'clock that day it had started snowing. We was out of anything to eat other than some coffee and cold biscuits. We finished them off and sent one of the boys with us back to the Tigre Mine to get some more supplies."

As though recalling the bitter cold wind that howled around the trees and rocks that day puts a fresh chill in his bones, Walter stands up and turns his backside to the fire. "We kept trying to move them cattle but by that time that snow storm was blowing a blizzard. We couldn't do anything with them cattle, couldn't drive them, nothing. They just wouldn't go. They kept turning their heads away from that snow and wind. Finally, we just tried to hold them together.

"Along about sundown we had them pretty well bunched up. The snow was about a foot deep or more on the ground and we hobbled most of our horses and figured the others would stay with them. There wasn't a stick of dry wood within ten miles. I guess it'd all been hauled into that Tigre Mine. We couldn't start a fire and we didn't have anything to eat so we just throwed our bedrolls off in that snow and crawled in.

"The next morning when we got up everywhere we looked there was cattle—out on this little point and over yonder and everywhere."

Walter chuckles and gestures off toward the shadowy corners of the room. "Horses the same way. This boy that had went to the Tigre had got caught in it and couldn't find his way back. He just tied his horse and two mules up and crawled in under an overhanging bluff. So that morning we didn't even have a cup of coffee. We just saddled up and started trying to get these cattle gathered. Along about noon that boy caught up with us. And about four o'clock that afternoon we finally got off the mountain with them cattle."

Walter stares into the fire and rubs at his knuckles. His hands seem a size too large for his body. Perhaps because he has used them the way other men use tools. "Right there was an old rock corral and a little old rock wall of a house that had a zacawiesta roof on it. Half of it was gone. But that day anything looked good. It was cold and the wind was blowing and we hadn't had a bite to eat all day—or even the night before. We got these cattle in the corral and patched it up to where we thought it would hold for the night. We got ourselves something to eat and put our beds under that old half of a roof.

"When we got up the next morning, the wind was still blowing, a little sleet in it, snow now and then. Just miserable. I was ready to turn these cattle out. But this partner of mine had disappeared. I thought, 'Well, I wonder where he's gone off to.' I wanted to get moving. I figured he'd show up directly. But he didn't come. I walked over to a bank that was about six feet high and looked over in there. There he was. He had his shirt and undershirt off and he was looking at hisself. I said, 'What're you doing?' And he said, 'I'm just lousier than a pet coon.' I guess he'd got them from sleeping under that old piece of grass roof. 'They ain't nothing I can do now,' he said. He just put his clothes back on and we pulled out."

Every day of this journey presented a new adventure. With the combination of cattle and weather there is always some crisis, something different and unexpected to deal with, which to Walter is simply the regular pattern of cowboy life. "We finally made it to the Bavispe River. It had been raining and snowing so much by then that that old river was really up. We got there maybe two hours before sundown and decided we'd better cross it before it got worse. We ran the cattle off into the water and got them started across." It was cold and the cowboys were not just damp anymore—they were soaked to the skin. "We had to go back across and get our horses and pack mules. Of course everything in our packs, our beds and everything, was soaking wet. By the time we got over with the cattle it started in to raining, just a cold rain. It was really pouring down."

Walter laughs now, though he does not recall laughing then. They were too miserable to be amused by anything. "There was a big old barn built there. We thought's we'd get in there and be dry if it didn't leak. We led our mules up to this old barn and was going to unpack when we heard something. There must've been twenty old hogs holed up in that barn, all bedded down and out of the rain.

"We proceeded to run them hogs out. It was pretty crazy. We'd run some out and when we'd go back to get the others them first ones would run back in. We finally got rid of them. I don't know where they went but we had their barn.

"From then on for the rest of that whole trip we slept in wet beds. And on the last day of February we finally rented a little old pasture over there within about fifty miles of where we wanted to go and turned them cattle loose. We went off and left them for a month. They had got so sorefooted that they just couldn't travel any further. Going all that distance in that wet weather over rocks and stuff and their feet was just wore out."

Walter watches the last of the fire, logs burnt down to char and beginning to break into little surface squares that give up a last breath of smoke. He's thinking about going down to the bunkhouse and turning in. In this shadowy light, the vestiges of each year, each branding, each roundup, and each hard drive down out of the mountains of Mexico can be read in Walter's face. And when he stands to leave, you see the shape all those years of being on horseback has given him and you realize he is still probably more comfortable riding than walking. He sets his hat just right and slips out into the dark.

Opposite: Jim Whiteker

They all talk about it. Somehow, no matter what question you ask, you hear this one thing at the heart of the answer. No one wants to name it, but it's something that exists at the very core of cowboy thinking.

After years of being around cowboys, of wanting to be one, and even trying out some parts of it, I have come to call this quality The Life. There is a loyalty to it that is, no matter how low-keyed it seems, fiercer than any loyalty to politics or a religion. In fact, many punchers who try to talk about certain aspects of their life end up almost calling it a religion; but to them it is a religion that is stronger, purer, and more rewarding than anything you find in a church, synagogue, temple, or tent.

Beth Wynn, who has lived on ranches in West Texas and East Central New Mexico, has observed this quality in her husband and sons. Just now finished with the breakfast dishes, she is drying her hands on the dish towel. "Everybody who lives in the country has a religious edge to their life," she says. "You go out and ride around the ranch and see so many things you just know there is a God up there. You couldn't help but have a special feeling about it. God is very real out here in the country."

Burl Wynn sits at the dining room table, listening to his wife talk. He works thoughtfully on a toothpick, rolling it to one corner of his mouth, keeping all but the tip of it inside. "I think most people that have worked around stock is religious to a certain extent," he agrees. "If you see a baby calf or a newborn colt or something, I think you know that there's somebody upstairs that's a little bigger than a man. That's the way I look at it. I don't think you have to run to church every time they open the doors up. I know I don't." He reaches up, pulls the toothpick from his mouth, and snaps it in two. "I think on the whole cowboys are maybe more religious than the man who lives in town."

Maybe they are. At any rate, they tend to look at religion in a little different light, holding it at a distance and not becoming self-conscious about it. As with everything else, punchers can see the humorous side. One afternoon, as I was

Opposite: Gary Green

95

driving with a couple of cowboys after working cattle on the Lewises' Turkey Creek Ranch somewhere in the vicinity of Bob Wills's hometown of Turkey, Texas, the subject of the cowboy's view of religion came up. One cowboy remembered a religious story about Harley Longan's youngest son, Jakie. It should be said here that Jakie is a big cowboy notorious for his sense of humor and love of good times. It seems that when he was about eight years old he went to Sunday School on Easter morning. The Sunday School teacher began talking about Christ, the crucifixion, the crown of thorns, the nails in his hands, the spear in his side, re-creating the whole scene for the kids in painful detail. At some point during the lesson she noticed that big tears were rolling down Jakie's cheeks. She stopped. "Jakie," she asked, "what's wrong?"

Jakie sniffed and cleared his throat, and said: "If Roy Rogers'd been there he'd have killed all those sonsofabitches—"

Some cowboys are regular churchgoers. More of them are not. Sometimes they will even deny that what they feel has anything to do with something that could be called religion. But most of the time it comes down to The Life. And when a cowboy like Jim Eicke talks about that, it sounds a lot like religion. "I'm not a religious person," Jim confesses. "I'm not a nonbeliever either. I believe there's somebody looking after us somewhere. But I don't go to church every Sunday and every Wednesday. We've got a thing called Cowboys for Christ. It's nondenominational. People give testimonies about what they've done and how it's changed their life. I've never given one yet." A big smile spreads over his face. "I don't think they're ready for mine. But we enjoy it and that's our way of being religious. I guess you'd call us Christian people. We try to live as good a life as we can."

We are in the comfortable living room at Casa Colorado. Jim looks around at his family. Jason has been picking the guitar quietly while he savors the pinch of snuff he slipped under his lip after supper. He leans and spits expertly into the small brass spittoon beside his boot. Pleased with what Jim just said, words she might have uttered herself, Sharon is smiling softly and looking at her hands. Shannon, who is ten, sits on the floor beside her dad's chair. She'd love a taste of Jason's Copenhagen, but she knows Jim wouldn't tolerate it. So she has to be content to sit and listen.

The room is quiet except for the soft murmur of the guitar, which somehow makes the silence more emphatic. Jim continues, "I don't believe I ever met a cowboy that if he was in a tight spot he wouldn't take his hat off and talk to whoever is up there. If he was in a bad way, in a wreck or a storm or something—he'd talk to the boss up there. And you know they're all pretty wild crazy old kids, most of them, when they're growing up. But they've all got respect. And if one of them wants to be real religious, nobody holds that against him. Because the biggest majority of people in this business they're a little closer to the Lord than ordinary people. I believe working out here does make you feel like that. Hell, you'd have to be when you look at all this. You wonder, who put that out there? Who made that so pretty? Who made all that country out there? Boy, the Lord sure done a good job."

Opposite and following page:
Branding, Walt Campbell Ranch

If it comes down to any one thing they can put their finger on to give it a name, it comes down to the land. The Lord and the land. And in this context the Lord is omnipotent and the land is all-inclusive; it includes everything that stands on it and emanates from it. Gary Loveland (and when he introduces himself, he says, "Love land," like that, in two words) believes a cowboy finds it in its pure state. "I lived in town a while after I was married and we had a couple of preachers come over—it ain't nothing against them or nothing—but they wanted you to go to church a lot and I figured I'm in the biggest church that the good Lord ever put on the earth—His country. I'm in His church seven days a week." But it wasn't something the preachers could either comprehend or abide.

When he hears the question, Roger Long frowns for a moment, as if it could be no question at all. "You get out here and look at all these things He's made, you know, and you can't hardly keep from being religious."

Louis Sanders, a young puncher from Caballo, New Mexico, a little town just south of Truth or Consequences, sums it up in three words: "Wide open spaces." He spreads his hands, almost helplessly, then goes on. "There hasn't always been churches. Older generations used to get out in the yard and worship. I do. I worship out in the open. When I see calves being born and grass growing and rain falling and everything I feel that I'm closer to the Lord than being in some church house. Don't get me wrong, I respect churches and everything. I'm just around His work all the time. I see it in the air, the trees, everything. I'd just sooner worship out here."

Somewhere in almost every conversation there is at least a hint to one of the reasons for this feeling of kinship with or closeness to "whoever is up there." Jim Whiteker mentions that he has one nagging fear of being alone; Jack Chatfield, who prides himself on his abilities as a breaker and trainer of horses, puts the same thing pretty succinctly: "I think every time a cowboy gets up in the morning he knows he may come back hung to his horse or he may not come back at all. That's there every day when you're punching cows. It could be one wrong turn of a cow. Your horse could step in a hole. Anything."

"Out here," Jim Whiteker insists, "a man is with himself and God. The first thing when you start to get in a wreck you think of all the wrongs you have done, and you're on the verge of a wreck all the time. You work with the crudest tools anybody could ever work with. You've got that constant element of danger. You're always flirting with that final danger. You can die out here."

Some people are more accident-prone than others. A man can take precautions. But to the thinking of many young punchers, at least, careful and cowboy are almost opposite terms. Part of being a cowboy is what it's always been: going at their work with almost total abandon. And yet, most of the men who survive do so more because of reason and pride than craziness and luck.

"I think you reap what you sow," Jim Whiteker concludes. "If you're sloppy it's going to tell on you. If a man lets things like his equipment go to pot he's asking for trouble. His girth can bust at a bad time and dump him under a running horse. He can break a rein. There's just always something waiting to happen."

It's true. Out here in God's country you can buy it easily. One wrong move at a critical moment, something unexpected to spook your horse, a gaping prairie dog hole he can't miss, a faulty bit of rigging that snaps—and it's all yours. It's a rare day on one of these places that at least one man doesn't bleed, blister, bruise, sprain, or break a bone; the cause can be a rope, a windmill, a strand of barbwire, a pickup, a horse, a cow, a snake, a spider, an act of God. Usually his comrades ignore it, as they are supposed to—until it is serious.

Many ranches are prepared for minor disasters. Over on the Bell, for example, a team from a Las Vegas hospital came in to give the hands—the camp men as well as all the single men down at the bunkhouse—a crash course in emergency first aid.

99

Castrating and branding, R.O. Ranch

A few of the cowboys' wives went on for more intensive training. Nobody wanted to take the time, but it paid off. Hardly a month had passed when Burl Wynn's horse fell with him and fractured his leg. Before driving him to the hospital the cowboys set the bones. The X rays revealed that they'd done a perfect job.

Danger is always there, inherent in the work, in everything they do and every move they make. Nobody is immune. Take Bert Ancell, a big, rawboned cowboy who looks, if anything, almost indestructible. One afternoon Bert threw his leg over a new bronc he was starting for his string and it came uncorked. When he hit the ground he heard the bone snap in his forearm. Then the very day he had the cast cut off he climbed on that same horse, was thrown again, and damned if he didn't break the other arm in almost the same place.

Thumbs and fingers can disappear in a furious flash. A puncher reaches out with his rope, catches a cow, calf, bull, or horse, takes a dally around his saddle horn, and something happens. There is a twist in the rope from a faulty coil, the horse shies or lunges unexpectedly, or the man is either too slow or careless, and the rope eats some flesh. It is ordinarily a painful, bloody mess. At best, there are long sessions in the emergency operating room, the surgeons trying to join up enough of the circulation system to make a successful regeneration possible. But more often than not the cowboy is left with a raw stub that never quite feels right.

Leo Turner, a puncher living in Double Adobe, Arizona, has spent more than fifty years working on big cattle ranches. Like most of his kind, Leo's had his share

of hard knocks. "But you know," he says, "the one thing that I think scared me the most was when I got hung to a horse there at the Bell Ranch. That was pretty wild. We had too many cattle in the corral and I was dragging calves. The horse I was dragging with was pretty spooky. He was a good horse, but he was afraid of a cow. We was nearly finished and the calves was getting pretty scattered. I went into the back of the corral and caught this calf. I started dragging him to the fire. There was too many cattle in there and they was milling. A great big old cow with big horns came around on the mill. She wasn't trying to charge this horse or nothing but he was afraid of her and he ducked back the wrong way. This pulled the rope over my back and I just knew I was starting to get in a heck of a wreck. I started to try and jump off of him. But I got all tangled up and fell on the rope that went under the horse. He kicked over it and I wound up right between his hind legs laying on my stomach across the rope."

Leo leans back in his chair, rubs a hand over his skull, and sighs. "Oh, he did really kick me, boogered me up something awful. He kicked me in the head and right back here on the spine. I imagine it'd been a whole lot worse if this Curtis Fort hadn't come over and cut my rope. That let me drop to the ground. It knocked me out. They had to haul me to Tucumcari. That's about the worst wreck I ever had."

Leo was lucky. Some men caught in the same situation don't survive. The horse keeps kicking and spinning and foundering; sometimes it falls on them, caving in their chest, breaking their neck, or crushing their skull. They are dragged to death by a bronc, battered by an incensed bull, trampled by a wild cow. They slip and fall from a windmill. Barbed wire pulled tight with the stretcher snaps and coils around them like the workings of a food processor. They are struck by lightning on a rainy hillside.

Sometimes they don't die. Sometimes they are only maimed and left to observe the life they wanted to live. They each have their story. Some of them tell it, some of them keep it inside.

Buck Ramsey is the former kind. In his forties and mercifully on the wagon these days, Buck is a gentle good man who once packed whole weeks of riotous cowboy living into a single day. People who knew Buck, who loved him, got to where they dreaded to see him. He could get wild and unruly and sweep them with him into binges of nightmarish proportions. Then, too, he ran with cowboys who were said to be both crazy and mean.

Nowadays, Buck is a whole lot tamer, saner. No matter how he disguises it with flashes of archaic cowboy lingo spoken in the broadest Panhandle twang that gives an extra stretch to most syllables, it is obvious that Buck is a bright and gifted man. He is philosophical and a storyteller of a different kind.

When Buck talks, he has a habit of saying something and then sort of sucking thoughtfully at his mouth and looking past you. His memory for certain key details can be vague, precise, or apocryphal, depending on his mood. Often, he will sprinkle his stories with quotations from such disparate sources as Shakespeare and Lyndon Johnson. In an attempt to sum up all of these qualities, one of his cowboy friends said to me, "Coming across Buck's just like finding a dime in a handful of old pennies."

Buck among his books in the Ramseys' house on Hayden Street in Amarillo is almost serene. In one corner of his study stands an old desk cluttered with newspapers, notes, and the various odds and ends of whatever he is currently working on. Buck sips at a Coke from the can, which is the way he always liked his booze, except when it came in bottles. His wife Betty sits at a table in the next room, sorting through some materials that have to do with her work in the school district.

Buck spent his early childhood out in the lush country along the Canadian River in the upper Panhandle. This was big ranch country, but unfortunately Buck's family were farmers. Right away he recognized the difference between farmers and cowboys and knew which he wanted to be. "I was just always struck by the way cowboys looked. There was something different about the way they carried themselves and the look in their eye."

Buck began to walk and talk cowboy, exactly the way he saw the punchers doing it. He worked on the ranches around his home and spent all the time he could with horses. He was learning and it was apparent that he had a natural ability for the work. Then, before he was out of high school, his family left the farm and moved to Amarillo. Buck was crushed. He had, however, developed a passion for

Jim Eicke

poetry and music, which didn't exactly go against the cowboy grain and which in its way kept him from being totally destroyed by having to live in town.

In the late fifties there was pressure to go to college, to get a degree. Buck tried. He day-worked as a cowboy and made a number of unsuccessful stabs at trying to adjust to the academic life. Eventually, he was kicked out of most of the colleges in West Texas, including Tech and Amarillo College. There were numerous reasons for his expulsions. Often it was for insolence, occasionally it was for

103

insolence added to a variety of more tangible things. Once, for instance, he drank all the whiskey he could hold and then painted a campus statue of Will Rogers bright blue. Why blue? He doesn't remember.

In the wake of that disaster, he decided he probably needed to travel. That was the panacea of the times. He wandered first to the West Coast and then to the East Coast, wearing his cowboy clothes and trying his hand at the poetry and music game. His only scores were rejections and disappointments.

When he looks back on it now he feels that he didn't have the sophistication to pull anything off in either field. But in those days he lacked any such overview. What he did to keep from starving to death was take a job carrying mail in a Rockefeller Center office building. And he read all of Camus, whose works he

Top: Scotty Anderson

Right: Robbie Seale

loved, except they only served to increase his frustration. "Then, too," he says, "in both California and New York I was assailed just a hell of a lot by homosexuals and I was beginning to get violent about that sort of stuff." So he came back to Texas, as he says, "looking for some green pastures and a place to get my head back in order."

The job he found taking care of a bunch of horses on a place east of Canyon, Texas, gave him enough free time to go back to school. He enrolled in West Texas State. He admits that his attitude had not changed but that something, some old guilt, continued to nag him to finish school. Again, he kept getting in trouble and being warned he'd be kicked out. He was doing okay reading and teaching himself different things but for some reason he couldn't cut it as a student. He'd go on a bender and be thrown in jail for fighting in some honkytonk around town and word

Leland Earle

of his being in jail would get back to the officials at the university.

"They didn't want bad young men in their nice school," he smiles. He pauses to sip on his Coke. "Dean Jones finally kicked me out of school. He said, 'You know, Buck, you're just like an old colt choking down. I know you're a good boy but you just keep choking down and choking down and you won't give any slack. We've just got to let you go. If you ever want to come back, you've got to come talk to me.'"

The next semester Buck decided to give it one more try. He put on a white shirt and pressed Levi's, shined his boots, and then went back to see Dean Jones.

The dean gave him a hard look. "Buck, are you really serious?"

"Yes, sir."

"What made you change your mind?"

"Well, Dean," he began, fighting the little dryness in his mouth, "I found the Lord and decided I wanted to be a preacher."

"Is that right, Buck?" The dean eyed him with suspicion. The white shirt, creased jeans, and the bit of boot polish were obviously helping his image and breaking down everything the dean remembered.

"Yes sir."

"I'm glad to hear it, Buck," the dean sighed. "Tell me how it happened."

Buck chuckles before going on. "I told him that a short time before I was ahorseback out under the trees and I remembered a day when me and my daddy were out milking cows and talking. We had been to church that day and my daddy was telling me what he wanted me to be when I grew up. I said, 'I was just out riding, remembering that, and I felt the hand of the Lord touch me.'"

Buck frowns, not without pleasure. It seems he had come to a point at which he had no alternative but to press on. "I finally ended up on my knees, praying. Dean Jones was crying by then and he told me through his tears that he was really glad that I was back. I said, 'Dean Jones, will you take just a moment and kneel down behind the desk with me and pray?' And I really laid a good old Baptist prayer on him." He sucks at his mouth for a second. "I made it through that semester— which was the only semester I did make it through."

School days were over. "I got through that deal and I didn't feel any different or any smarter; it wasn't doing anything to me, for me, or anything. I knew now that I could do it and somehow that was enough. I just decided that from then on I'd rather be ahorseback out there."

Buck went to work for the Whittenburgs, on a ranch they had out of Stinnett, north of the Canadian River. "Betty had been chasing me," he says, smiling and raising his voice enough so she can hear him. "Got her a job at Borger, which was pretty close. She started vamping me pretty strong so I married her while I was out there. They didn't have a good married camp on that place so I moved onto the Bivins Ranch. A nice old camp. It was the real McCoy. My life quieted down a whole lot. I wasn't getting to town very often."

Buck's tone changes, just perceptibly, just enough to let me know that recalling the subject still brings him some pain. "I was over at the Bivins when I got

Opposite: Gary Loveland and
Douglas Johnson

106

hurt. The foreman there hired me out to ride his rough stock, to ride his broncs. And he had a bunch of those old spoiled horses that he wanted me to try and do something with. They ought to just send them to the soap factory when they get spoiled like that. Spoiled, dishonest damned horses." Buck shakes his head, frowning. "There were two or three that I knew would never be any good. I avoided them. I just didn't want to mess with them. The foreman cornered me one day and asked why I wasn't riding any of them. I told him it wasn't because they bucked or anything like that. They were just too spoiled, too dishonest."

It wasn't exactly fear that kept him off those broncs. It was simply that he didn't feel like wasting his time on them. But the day came when he did saddle up one of the worst of that spoiled bunch and decided to put some miles on him. "There were three or four of us leaving the corral. I closed the gate. I stepped up on this horse and he started to buck before my foot even hit the stirrup. Finally, I did get my stirrup and I was riding him real good. There was a kind of slope going down to a dry creek bed. It was about three hundred yards away. He bucked all the way down there and got into that sand. You know how a horse will lunge when he gets in soft sand or water. He started to lunge like that and the shank broke off the hackamore. It was a sorry old bear-trap kind of hackamore rig the foreman thought would work on that horse. I lost my balance. I was losing my stirrups and he lunged again real hard. I had hold of the saddle horn and he just kind of shot me into the creek embankment. It broke my spine." Buck stops for a second, then he says, "That was the end of my cowboying."

Buck gives his wheelchair a shove, letting it roll slowly into the middle of the floor. I no longer hear Betty shuffling through her papers in the next room. Is she listening for Buck to go on?

There is more to the story. Another puncher filled me in. It seems the cowboys who were riding with Buck thought the best thing was to get him to the hospital as fast as they could. So they loaded him into the back of a pickup and he was jolted all the way to town. At the hospital, the doctors figured that it was the drive that finally caused his spine to be completely severed and the damage to be permanent. But, then, maybe there really is no more to that story—at least not for Buck.

Opposite: Johnny and Karen Hill

On the north side of Rob Groves's house at the Frying Pan, one of the Marsh ranches west of Amarillo, Texas, an old man and a boy are practice-roping a plastic steer head. Squinting just enough to transform it into serious sport, they build their loops and take turns throwing at the head. The little boy, Rob's grandson, is called T.J. and the old man is J.C. King. T.J. swings his rope and comes in close, crouching, then lets the loop fly. He crows when it snags one horn. J.C., an expert both in the branding corral and the rodeo arena, which are two different and distinct kinds of roping, throws a smaller loop that sails out flat and neat, the stiff hemp circling over the black horns and cracking against the black PVC.

J.C., who "retired" a few years back, always seems to be on hand when there is a branding or shipping; and the rest of the time he's off on the Old Timer's Rodeo circuit somewhere, knocking down his share of the day money and winning solid silver trophy buckles as big as pie plates. Staying busy doing the thing he liked best is J.C.'s idea of the only kind of retirement he could ever possibly imagine.

All through the early evening, Rob's friends and neighbors keep either phoning or showing up in pickup trucks to make sure the branding is on for the next day. Marion Kinsey will be down from the Dripping Springs Ranch. H. Barnard and his grandson Chris will be here. Billy Spears is coming, and a couple of Mexicans from another Marsh ranch, as well as half a dozen other punchers. If they have driven over, then they stomp into the kitchen, cup their hands around tall plastic tumblers of iced tea, prop their elbows on the oil cloth that covers the table, and talk with Rob.

These cowboys are separated by miles of fenced range and farmland and by the constant work it takes to keep their ranches running, and this first branding of the year is both an opportunity to get together and an excuse to catch up on all they've missed.

While he still does basically what he always did—take care of cattle—the way a cowboy does it has in many respects changed significantly. Once, of course, the

Opposite: Louis and Floyd Sanders

111

Jenks and Bobby Boston

variety was greater. Shipping was vastly different. There were massive roundups where the herds from a number of ranches running on the same range would be gathered, sorted, and counted; and then they were driven in huge herds to a shipping point. The invention of barbed wire in 1873 by an Illinois farmer named Joseph Glidden (his patent is dated November 24, 1874) made it possible for ranchers to contain their herds and thus changed the whole scope of not only the roundup but of the entire cattle business. And eventually the railroads sent their lines deep into cattle country, making the long trail drives up into the midwest no longer necessary; and finally the building of roads and the use of cattle trucks put an end to almost any kind of drive.

One thing that has remained almost as it was from the beginning is branding. It is pure cowboy work. And punchers, even the loners, look forward to it. That

George Winkley III

underlying tone of anticipation is something I hear in the voices that continue in the kitchen until just before midnight, when I fall asleep.

My alarm has not yet gone off when the headlights of the first trucks flash across the yard and the dogs start to bark. Coffee is made, the sharp smell permeating the house. These days always begin in the dark. The men finish breakfast and drive to the pasture in order to be mounted before sunup. The windmills, motionless on the horizon, have the stark, black look of a sketch and the air seems somehow too cold and brisk for Texas. In fact, at this moment, the only promise of any warmth in the coming hours is in the absolute cloudlessness of the sky. The riders fan out, each one knowing his position, knowing just how far and fast to ride, and they begin the task of gathering the pasture and bringing the cattle to the pens.

Two hours later, in the full sun, the lowing of the approaching cattle is sudden and strong. You hear their voices first, even before you see the dust that rises above the moving cows and calves. The sound has a strange quality; it gathers and becomes somehow stronger without being particularly louder, only closer and more distinct.

The riders drive the herd into the corrals. They cut out the bulls and dry cows, shunting them into a separate pen. Seeing these horses at work, you understand immediately the "cow" a puncher talks about in a well-bred cow pony. Once they are shown the animal to be cut out they stay with it until they have separated it from the others. They are quick and they work with an astonishing concentration. And once they have the cow or calf where it belongs and the rider gives a signal that the cut is over the horse calms down immediately, ready to slip back into the herd.

Rob Groves, his battered black hat tugged over a wind-reddened face, starts the fire and thrusts a handful of branding irons into the flame. Chock, the cowboy who works with Marion Kinsey on the Dripping Springs place, begins to draw the blade of his pocket knife across a whetstone, honing it razor-sharp for the castrating. Rob's son Robbie fills a syringe with antibiotics. The cowboy called simply H. holds the dehorning tool against a fence post and takes the rust off its circular edges with a file. J.C. King and Billy Spears tighten their cinches, ready to rope and drag the slick, or unbranded, calves to the fire.

I realize that among eight of the ten cowboys waiting for the branding irons to show enough color to sear the Frying Pan brand into the hides of the calves there is, collectively, something like four centuries of experience in gathering, branding, dehorning, and castrating cattle. And nothing about any of what's going on here would suggest the shuffleboard court or bingo table in a senior citizens' center, where men younger than these by a decade or more seek out ways to dispel boredom and fill up their last years.

Sons and grandsons watch with respect while punchers in their late sixties and seventies swing easily up into the saddle, undo their ropes, snake out a loop, and bring a calf bawling and kicking to the fire. In each practiced loop they cast one recognizes a kind of finished pride. It is not ostentatious, but it is there. These are veterans of the profession, cowboys who have gone along with the changes in the life and ridden out the worst storms and upheavals that have hit the business. They have today, as they've doubtlessly had each year of their lives, a fresh enthusiasm for the work they are here to do.

There is an art to it all. And it is in the art that the men take their pride. Two crews work, one on each side of the fire. In a smaller pen with a smaller crew, as I have seen at Walt Campbell's ranch a hundred miles south of here or on the Steve Trigg ranch out of Logan, New Mexico, there will be only one crew. But the pattern is always pretty much the same as it always has been.

The ropers, J.C. King and Billy Spears, ease their horses into the herd, single out a calf, pick up the hind legs with a loop, take a wrap around the saddle horn with the rope, and start for the fire. The flankers function together, one grabbing

the rope, the other taking the tail, to throw the calf to the ground. The men here, accustomed to branding with one another, make it look simple. Instead of trying to muscle a calf to the ground, good flankers employ a rhythm that incorporates momentum, the movement of the calf, and their combined weight to get the animal on the ground. One flanker places his knee on the calf's neck. His partner sits down, still grasping the tail, releases the rope, and then takes hold of one hind leg and stretches it out straight to keep the calf from kicking. Robbie Groves injects the animal in the neck. Rob earmarks him, cutting notches from his ears that, with the brand, serve as identifying marks. Marion Kinsey, who is brander for this first bunch, brings the iron from the fire and applies it. The hair bursts into flame and sends up smoke in an acrid white cloud. H. takes the dehorning tool and in a firm, circular motion digs the two short horn nubs out of the calf's skull. Chock slices off the tip of the scrotum, pulls out both testicles, and cuts them off. The entire process is over in not much more than a minute and the calf is turned loose to head back into the herd and find his mother.

The little cod ends are put in a pile for the final tally—to tell how many steers are among the calves. The testicles are kept in a bucket, to be cleaned and served up as the seasonal delicacy known as calf fries in this part of the country and as Rocky Mountain oysters in other places.

There is something almost ritualistic about calf fries. Sometime in the middle of the morning, a couple of the older cowboys will thread a few on a strand of baling wire and roast them over the open flame. But most of them will be kept for later—to be soaked in buttermilk, coated with batter, and deep-fried. That is the basic preparation. Every calf fry fanatic has his own carefully guarded recipe, some variation on the preparation for the soaking, secret ingredients for the batter, or something about the way they are fried that is guaranteed to make them the best I've ever tasted. To some men taste is only part of it—significant, of course, but not everything. They believe the calf fry has an amazing range of properties and benefits that includes everything from being an aphrodisiac to an elixir.

To keep everything moving smoothly and give different cowboys a chance at roping and dragging, the men rotate from job to job. They work quickly, seriously, but not without humor. The gibes because of a missed loop, a good thrashing from a particularly difficult calf, are part of the day. Men with this much experience make the job look easy and seem determined to keep it from appearing as if anyone is really working that hard. It is part of the style, the universal cowboy temperament, the nonchalance that goes with the breed. Almost nothing is so tough that it can't have a light side. At the end of a hard day's branding on one of the Lewis ranches, Frank Derrick, the manager, called to one of the cowboys, "Billy, can you get a count on this pen?" Another cowboy piped up in a dry voice, "If there's more than ten head, he'll have to take off his boots first."

Sometime before noon, Rob's daughter Jo Angela, the mother of T.J., rides out to the pens. She has been helping her mother, Jo Rita, fix the dinner. Now that it is all under control she wants to help with the branding. Rob hands her the syringe and takes T.J. over to the fence, where they sit and watch together.

J.C. King, who has given up his roping job to Chock, chuckles and nods toward Jo Angela. "She's as good a hand as any man here. She's got a real way with a horse."

It is almost one o'clock when the last of the slick calves are finally branded. Then the whole herd is sprayed with insecticide. The cowboys get back in the saddle and, moving more slowly in the midday heat, drive the herd back to the pasture. They load their horses into the trailers that were parked at the head of the pasture before dawn and return to the house.

Dinner is a big, substantial meal. Most of the men go back to the buffet set up in the kitchen for seconds. They linger out in the yard, sitting in groups, talking, listening. I find myself watching one young puncher. He hasn't said a single word since morning and I've never heard his name. He sits near a circle of men who've relaxed on the lawn. Sometimes they glance his way, including him in the conversation, which is about a rustler who had been caught the previous summer somewhere out between Amarillo and the Canadian River, but it is obvious that they don't expect him to participate. I question another puncher about him. The man shrugs. "He don't have nothing to say." It's that simple.

There is, it seems, a reluctance to leave. And indeed you do get a kind of hollow feeling when you see the last pickup and gooseneck horsetrailer spin out of the yard and start up the hill in a cloud of dust.

Only J.C. King has stayed. There is no real reason. He could drive back into Amarillo and put up his horses. But there are a few hours of the afternoon left and he'd a whole lot sooner spend them out here, in the kind of country where he lived most of his life. Besides, he figures it won't hurt to make use of this time and get in a little more practice. He breaks out the rope he uses in the rodeo arena, taking it from the special round tin container that keeps it coiled just so, builds a loop, swings it twice around his head, and drops it precisely over the black horns of the PVC dummy.

When he retrieves the rope, winding neat coils into his left hand, shaking out a new, perfect loop with his right, there is a distant look in his eyes. Watching him, I wonder where his thoughts are—on the next Old Timer's Rodeo, or somewhere in the past when today's branding would have marked only the beginning of a long season on whatever ranch he was then working. Suddenly the loop is singing through the air; it drops with a furious accuracy over the fake horns and J.C. snaps up the slack.